In this fine shot of the first
production L-1049 Super
Connie (c/n 4001) registered
N6201C, the elongated
fuselage has retained its
beautifully contoured form.
This particular aircraft entered
service with Eastern Air Lines
on 15 December 1951 and was
given the fleet No 201.
Lockheed

Classic Civil Aircraft:1
LOCKHEED CONSTELLATION

KENNETH E. WIXEY

IAN ALLAN
Publishing

Acknowledgements

I should like to express my gratitude to the following companies and individuals without whose generous help this book would have remained a project only:

The Lockheed California Co for its exceptional assistance and advice, especially Robert C. Ferguson; Shirley Lee (Trans World Airlines); Peter Joel (Pan American World Airways); Ken Groves and John J. White (QANTAS); Christine Howarth (Lufthansa); Bob Harris (Air France), Rod Barlow (KLM); Lizzan Peppard (Aer Lingus); Martin Thompson (Northwest Orient); Guilherme Tully (VARIG SA); Jane Whigham (Air Canada); the Public Relations Departments of Air India International, Eastern Air Lines and Swissair.

I am indebted to the following for permission to use their photographs: Brian Pickering (Military Aircraft Photographs); Quadrant Picture Library (Flight International) and Roger P. Wasley.

Finally, but by no means least, I am grateful to Peter J. Marson and Air Britain for permission to glean certain information from their massive tome devoted to the Constellation, a volume I can recommend to anyone wishing to further their research into registrations, construction numbers (c/n) and individual Constellation histories.

First published 1987
This impression 1998

ISBN 0 7110 1735 2

© Ian Allan Ltd 1987, 1998

Published by Ian Allan Publishing

an imprint of Ian Allan Ltd, Terminal House, Station Approach, Shepperton, Surrey TW17 8AS.

Contents

Printed by Ian Allan Printing Ltd at its works at Coombelands in Runnymede, England.

Code: 9804/A

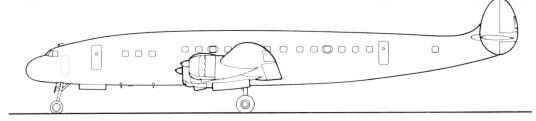

Introduction

According to the well known adage, 'beauty is in the eye of the beholder', and in the case of the Lockheed Constellation airliner this was particularly true. To many people the Constellation, or 'Connie' as she became affectionately known, was the most aesthetically pleasing four-engined piston aeroplane to ever reach quantity production. Others considered the Constellation as merely another passenger-carrying transport aircraft with an unusually distinctive profile.

Whatever the view taken on the Constellation, however, there is no doubt that it was a magnificent and extremely aerodynamically efficient aeroplane. Certainly it was deserving of the accolades bestowed upon it, and must surely rank among the all-time greats in aviation history.

When it was originally introduced the Constellation was intended for civil use, but World War 2 was then some three years old and the United States Army Air Force (USAAF) grabbed the type for fast transport duties. They found the Connie could exceed the speed of some versions of the Japanese Mitsubishi A6M Zero fighter, was faster than any contemporary four-engined bomber and had the capability to airlift an armoured fighting vehicle nonstop over long distances.

In the climate of postwar civil aviation, development of the Constellation continued apace and a number of civil and military variants emerged including the 'stretched' Super Constellation. This was later complemented by the ultimate design in the Constellation series, the Starliner. This very much updated version was, unfortunately, soon ousted from service with the major airlines by the new generation of jet airliners entering service.

Replacements of all types in the Constellation series became increasingly rapid as jetliners took over the services on the more important world airline routes. Constellations, Super Constellations and Starliners were relegated to secondary duties, operating with less significant airlines. Quite a number ended up as freighters and became an asset to small operators, especially in Latin American countries. Other machines quickly became redundant and sadly fell before the breakers' torch. Before their demise, however, the Constellation family had carried many thousands of passengers comfortably, safely and speedily to destinations all over the world with airlines great and small.

This then is its story, and it is the writer's intention that this book be regarded as a tribute to the Constellation in all her forms, a classic aeroplane and probably the most elegant and successful piston-engined airliner with four engines ever built in the United States.

Kenneth E. Wixey
Brockworth
May 1986

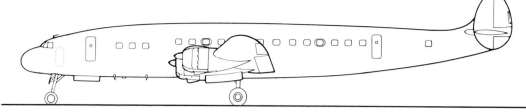

1 Background and Concept

The Lockheed Constellation was, technically and aerodynamically, a great innovation in the transport of passengers by air. It was the result of advanced ideas and the combined expertise of what appeared to be a comparatively young company. However, this same organisation, the Lockheed Aircraft Corp, owed its origins to two brothers way back in 1913. In San Francisco Malcolm and Allan Loughead (pronounced Lockheed) had designed and constructed a floatplane during that year which they called their Model G, and for a number of years this machine was used to convey passengers on pleasure flights in the area and later at Santa Barbara.

By 1916 the brothers had founded the Loughead Aircraft Manufacturing Co at Santa Barbara, and had taken into their employ an aircraft designer by

the name of John K. Northrop. The company intended to design and produce a twin-engined flying boat for service with the US Navy, but this did not materialise and, during the remaining years of World War 1, Loughead were responsible for the modification and construction of Curtiss flying boats under contract. After the war the company attempted to continue with their aircraft business by producing a small sporting biplane, but this venture

Below:
This 1929 aerial view shows the original premises leased to the Lockheed Aircraft Co at Burbank. High-wing Vega monoplanes are predominant among the newly-built aircraft that can be seen outside the buildings. *Lockheed*

came to nothing and the Loughead concern temporarily vanished from the aviation scene.

In 1926 Allan Loughead and John Northrop formed the Lockheed Aircraft Co. Northrop later departed to start up on his own, but he left behind him the legacy of the famous Vega high-wing monoplanes, one of which, *Winnie Mae*, became famous in the early 1930s when Wiley Post and Harold Gatty made their record-breaking round-the-world flights. Northrop's place at Lockheed was taken by Gerald Vultee who created a number of well known Lockheed types which included the Altair and Orion. The Lockheed Orion was the first commercial production aircraft to incorporate a retractable undercarriage and the first in this class to possess a top speed in excess of 200mph. The development of civil aviation in the 1930s owes much to the Orion, especially the smaller airlines, for with its superb performance and relatively economical running costs this single-engined low-wing monoplane helped to firmly establish a number of embryo airlines. Among them were CMA/Mexicana, Aerovias Centrales and Lineas Aereas Mineras SA (LAMSA) in Mexico, Bowen Airlines in the USA and Swissair in Europe.

Meanwhile, having established themselves as a successful manufacturer of civil aeroplanes, Lockheed decided to move to Burbank, California. Then came the depression of the 1930s and the Lockheed Co, which had become a division of the Detroit Aircraft Corporation (affiliated to the giant US motor car industry), found itself in financial difficulties. However, with the help of a fresh management team which possessed a great knowledge of aviation and its contemporary requirements, the Lockheed Aircraft Co, as it became known, survived to embark on a revised design and construction programme for a new generation of twin-engined transport aircraft. These included the Model 10A Electra, 12A, 14 Super Electra (from which evolved the military version known as the Hudson) and the Model 18 Lodestar. In addition there was later to emerge the twin-boom P-38 Lightning, a long range single-seat fighter.

Needless to say, productivity on this scale demanded substantial amounts of both capital and

Right:
Seen in its drab camouflage, this Lockheed 10A was operated by the RAF on communications duties during World War 2. It was one of three impressed for UK service (W9104-W9106) and flew with No 24 Squadron. *MAP*

Centre right:
The twin-engined Hudson bomber gave Lockheed their first big export order in 1938. This L-214 Mk 1 Hudson, having just arrived in the UK, has had its Boulton & Paul dorsal gun turret fitted in readiness for service with RAF Coastal Command. *MAP*

Below:
Evolved from the earlier Lockheed 10, the 12-seat Model 14 Super Electra proved a sound basis for the Hudson bomber, while the updated 14-seat version became the Model 18 Lodestar. This picture shows Lodestar NC25636 in service with Continental Airlines c1940. *MAP*

Some other manufacturers thought Lockheed unwise to take on the Hudson order with their limited facilities, but the company president Robert E. Gross was confident it could be done, and he told his workforce of 2,500 so in December 1938. The British contract for up to a maximum of 250 Hudsons was worth a possible $25 million to the company and Gross was determined to fulfil his promise. Fortunately the vice-president of the California Bank, Charles A. Barker Jr, joined Lockheed as vice-president of the company in charge of finances. Almost immediately he and Gross invaded the credit market by raising $1.25 million in short-term funds, this amount being supplemented by a $3 million stock issue early in

space, and Lockheed was aware that for the level of production it anticipated the available facilities were inadequate. Because it leased its property, the management were at first reluctant to invest in modernising buildings and plant which it did not own, but late in 1936 the decision was taken to purchase both land and buildings to facilitate aircraft production.

As a result of that important step involving what was to become known as the B-1 factory at Burbank, plus some 43 acres and about 108,000sq ft of plant, new capital would have to be raised. Added to this was the development costs of the latest Model 14 twin-engined transport. Efforts to substantially increase Lockheed's assets included two stock issues which brought in $1.6 million. Much of this went into new buildings and the installation of updated machinery and equipment, while a new administration centre together with an engineering office was erected, thus by 1938 production facilities had doubled with 250,000sq ft of floor space being available. This was at the time when the large British order for Hudson reconnaissance bombers had been accepted, and Lockheed's working capital was some $650,000, with $334,000 actually in the company's bank.

1939. The Lockheed Aircraft Corp was thus destined to become a member of the big league in the manufacture of civil and military aircraft, for the 250th Hudson was rolled out 7½ weeks ahead of schedule, resulting in further contracts involving nearly 3,000 Hudsons.

In the meantime the company had been toying with the idea of a four-engined passenger-carrying aircraft, this being some time prior to the conception of the Constellation. A design project was put forward known as the Model 44 Excalibur, and this was enlarged upon when Pan American Airways (PAA) suggested a pressurised version capable of carrying up to 40 passengers. In its revised form it was envisaged that the projected airliner would be fitted with a nosewheel, weigh some 40,000lb gross, cruise at 250mph at an altitude of 12,000ft and have a range somewhat less than that of the contemporary Boeing 307 Stratoliner.

In June 1939 another airline, Transcontinental & Western Air (TWA), decided to approach Lockheed about its requirements for an aeroplane that would show a marked improvement over the Boeing 307,

TWA already being involved with that type at the time. Those present at the meeting were Howard Hughes, financial head of TWA, the airline's president Jack Frye, Lockheed's president Robert E. Gross, and the company's engineering representatives Hall L. Hibbard and Clarence L. 'Kelly' Johnson. TWA wanted an aircraft with a longer range, faster speed and higher altitude capability than the Boeing 307 Stratoliner. They proposed a machine which could carry a 6,000lb payload, cruise at between 250 and 300mph at an altitude approaching 20,000ft, and accommodate a crew of six for the flight deck and cabins. In response Lockheed took a hard look at their Project 44 design and, although this could not be considered as the actual progenitor of their Model 49 design (or Excalibur A as it was known before being renamed Constellation), it provided a basis upon which to work.

The initial problem to be overcome concerned the size and type of powerplant, calculations making it apparent that very large engines would be the most suitable for this type of aeroplane. These findings were based on figures relating to the

efficiency of large aero-engines running at a low percentage of their power rating, with a minimum amount of supercharging. In smaller engines there was a weight-saving factor of 1,385lb, although more complex supercharging was required and they would be capable of the performance demanded, but the weight-saving advantage was lost after the distance flown exceeded 755 miles. The advantages of the larger engines then became apparent as the range increased. For example, as the more powerful engines carried additional payload, it was calculated that given a range of 2,500 miles the effective payload would exceed 3,000lb. There were other advantages, too, in using the larger engines: improved take-off capability, a higher safety margin, less complicated powerplant installation, greater reliability through the use of low cruising power and a much better maximum performance.

The choosing of a suitable engine for Lockheed's new design was not difficult. For a number of years the Curtiss-Wright organisation had been producing a successful series of air-cooled radial engines including the Whirlwind and Cyclone. Development of the latter had by now resulted in a double-row 18-cylinder affair, the Wright R-3350-745C18BA-1 Cyclone 18. This produced 2,200hp for take-off, a cruise rating of 1,400hp at 14,000ft, and its fuel consumption figure was less than that of the earlier R-2600 Cyclone 14. Thus Lockheed decided to power their new Model 49 design with four Cyclone 18s, an engine which, in its progressive forms, would be adopted as the standard powerplant for all models of the Constellation.

It was decided that to minimise the drag effect of the four big radials, a reverse-flow cowling design should be considered and this was consequently produced and taken for wind tunnel tests in one of six wind tunnel facilities, as indeed were all major components of the Model 49. Most wind tunnel tests on the Constellation were undertaken at the University of Washington and in the Lockheed Aerodynamic Laboratory. Some tests were, however, carried out at the California Institute of Technology, or with the National Advisory Committee for Aeronautics (NACA) which possessed three wind tunnels, one each for high speed and spinning tests, and a third (a 19ft affair) for general testing.

To facilitate development of a proper engine installation for the L-49, Lockheed produced a large-scale model nacelle incorporating a 30hp motor. This enabled the company to try out not only the reverse flow cowling but also a variety of standard type cowlings. It was consequently proved during the tests that the reverse flow cowling proposal was not particularly efficient. The incoming cooling air passing backwards to the engine by induction via slots in the wing leading-edge, had to be exhausted behind the large propeller spinner while the reversal of the airflow twice through 180° contributed much to a substantial internal flow loss, which was not compensated for by the lower basic nacelle drag of the streamlined units. Other experiments were tried out, one featuring blowers built into the spinners, but it was eventually decided that a standard type of straight-through cowling would be best suited to the L-49 design.

Lockheed's engineers headed by Clarence L. 'Kelly' Johnson and Hall L. Hibbard were now faced with the awesome task of formulating an optimum airframe to which these, by contemporary standards, massive engines could be applied. Their aim in accordance with the conception was a long range, high altitude, high speed transport for which the basic requirement was low operating costs. At the same time it was to be an aeroplane in which flight characteristics must be a substantial improvement over its contemporaries with maximum controllability available for emergency as well as normal flight conditions.

Left:
An interior view of the wind tunnel at Lockheed's Aerodynamic Laboratory in which a model of the more advanced L-1649 Starliner with laminar flow wing is prepared for tests. *Lockheed*

Right:
A recent portrait of Clarence L. 'Kelly' Johnson, the man principally responsible for engineering and developing numerous Lockheed aircraft types including the entire Constellation family. *Lockheed*

2 Design and Development

Initially planned to incorporate cabin pressurisation, air refrigeration and the air conditioning of fumes and humidity in its design, the L-49 had also to conform to Amendment 56 of the Civil Air Regulations transport flight requirements regarding the ability to operate safely from small airfields. In order to comply with this regulation, while at the same time carrying the heaviest possible load, it was essential that a high overall lift coefficient must be obtained for the aircraft. At that time the most effective flap for this purpose was the Lockheed-Fowler type as used on the Model 14 and Hudson, which resulted in a modified version of this flap being produced and tested in the wind tunnel.

When fitted to the Constellation the flaps created increased problems with the landing performance, especially with elevator control and the effects of aileron control when two engines on the same side were inoperative.

Rudder control presented another problem due to the large engines being employed in a relatively small airframe. Lockheed's previous experience with twin vertical tail surfaces had revealed that, when directional stability was less important than directional control, multiple fins and rudders had an advantage over the single unit. This was not so true in aircraft with much less power where the single fin and rudder was preferred because of its lighter weight and less complex structure. In the case of the L-49, triple fins and rudders were chosen, but because of the effects of slipstream from the airscrews the necessarily large horizontal tailplane had to be fitted on the upper rear fuselage, the camber line of which was raised. With two inset fins and rudders and a third on the fuselage centreline, the arrangement required little trim when the aircraft's flaps and landing gear were down.

Below:
The starboard Lockheed-Fowler flap on this rather weather-beaten Hudson Mk III, BW450 of the RCAF, can plainly be seen in its partly lowered position. *MAP*

Maximum controllability of all movable flying surfaces on such a large aeroplane as the Constellation was the next problem to overcome if minimum control speeds and other basic advantages were to be obtained. It had already been decided from the start that the most practical answer was the incorporation of hydraulic boosters for all controls, but this was not easy. Apart from the extremely difficult technicalities involved, there was the problem of objections from officialdom regarding the installation of complicated mechanisms as a substitute for the already well proven control cable systems prevalent on most contemporary aircraft types. A compromise was reached, however, whereby the hydraulic booster system was complemented by standby units for emergency use.

Lockheed had in fact been involved with the development of hydraulic control surface boosters in 1939 before design work on the Constellation began, but the decision to incorporate this type of controllability into the L-49 was finalised only after a thorough investigation of all the factors involved. It was found that the advantages of control surface boosters far outweighed the disadvantages, but as there were no existing values upon which to work in regard to what control forces pilots wanted on a large aircraft, Lockheed produced a number of units with variable boost ratios.

As a result of several pilots undertaking a considerable amount of flying time on the project, a set of figures was drawn up which could be used for the Constellation's control surface boosters. Critical control conditions investigated to obtain this result included landing at minimum control speed with two engines feathered and approaches in turbulent air. This study in comfortable and suitable control loadings was to result in basic requirement figures thus: with elevator at full deflection the desirable force on the wheel was 50-80lb (maximum obtainable 160lb); rudder at full deflection — 150lb on the pedal (maximum obtainable 500lb); aileron partially deflected — desirable force of 10ft/lb (maximum obtainable 35ft/lb right and 30ft/lb left). Although elevator forces down to 35lb were tried out in some landings, they proved too light. On the Constellation these desirable forces were obtained with the exception of the ailerons with which it was difficult to attain the required figure because of a 5-6ft/lb friction factor in the system.

To achieve such results was not simple, a fact better realised perhaps when it is understood that the horizontal tailplane of the Constellation was greater in area by 10sq ft than the wing area for a Lockheed 10A Electra, or nearly half that of a Douglas DC-3 wing. It is obvious, therefore, that a substantial boost ratio would be necessary to move a quarter of this area through a 40° arc at an airspeed of 90mph with a desired force of 80lb.

Such a large elevator was a necessity on the Constellation because of the design requirement that the type should have the ability to use small airfields, a factor which would result in higher payloads being carried from more places. This of course meant that exceptionally good control was necessary where the elevator, rudder and ailerons had to operate under very critical conditions. Additionally with such powerful engines, when one was feathered the rudder and aileron control problem was greater than that of other transport aircraft at a given airspeed. This was mainly due to the distance between the fuselage and engines and because of the necessarily large diameter of the propellers. Thus to provide optimum landing characteristics the use of a powerful elevator was essential.

In the event the final boost ratios arrived at for the L-49 Constellation were much higher than those for other types of aircraft, which usually worked out at something like 3:1 or 4:1. The Constellation's figures were: elevator 9.33:1, rudders 23:1 and the ailerons 26:1, these ratios being made practicable through the use of a small amount of servo action on trim tabs, this having no adverse effect on drag, area or weight factors.

The next stage in the development was to construct a full-scale layout in Lockheed's laboratory of the complete hydraulic system involving the boosters, landing gear, flaps, pumps, the whole pipework installation, automatic pilot, brakes and a cockpit mock-up. Everything was measured to fit in the exact position it would take up on the actual aeroplane, and from the cockpit were controlled four engines built by the Ford Motor Co which simulated the aero-engines and provided the impetus for the hydraulic pumps. Flaps and landing gear were both subjected to simulated air loads, while the elevators, rudders and ailerons underwent actual air load conditions through the use of huge springs, the load figures themselves having been arrived at after wind tunnel tests. To ensure that the differing speed ranges of the L-49 were tested under load conditions, a programme was arranged in which the loads expected to occur at 80, 120, 200 and 350mph were reproduced. Other stringent tests involved the freezing of the entire tail unit to −70°F after which the controls were operated, the forces working on them being measured with the object of studying the effect of very low temperatures on the hydraulic booster system. There was also a contamination test in which dirt and water were deliberately added to the hydraulic fluid, the system then being run at normal and low temperatures.

The reason for the distinctive serpentine contours of the Constellation's fuselage was not simply for good looks. The large 15ft diameter propellers meant that an extremely long travel was necessary

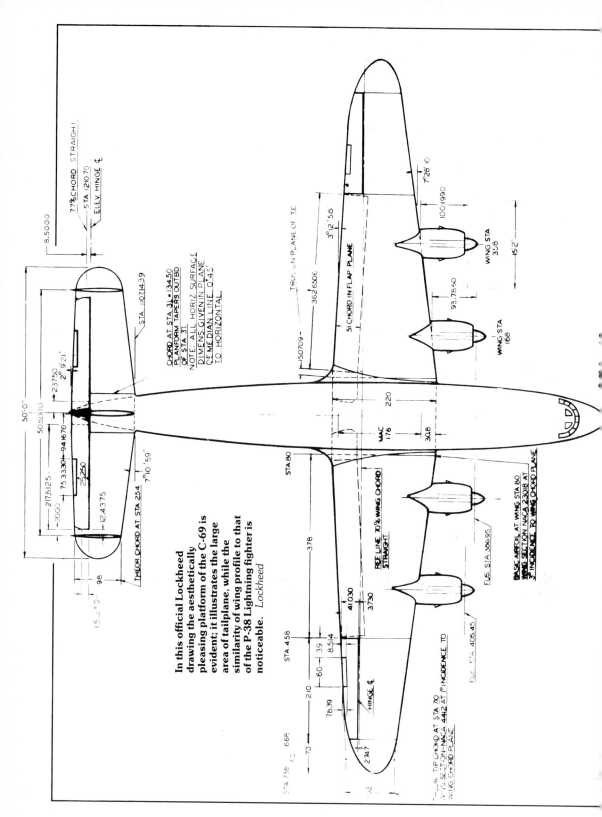

In this official Lockheed drawing the aesthetically pleasing platform of the C-69 is evident; it illustrates the large area of tailplane, while the similarity of wing profile to that of the P-38 Lightning fighter is noticeable. *Lockheed*

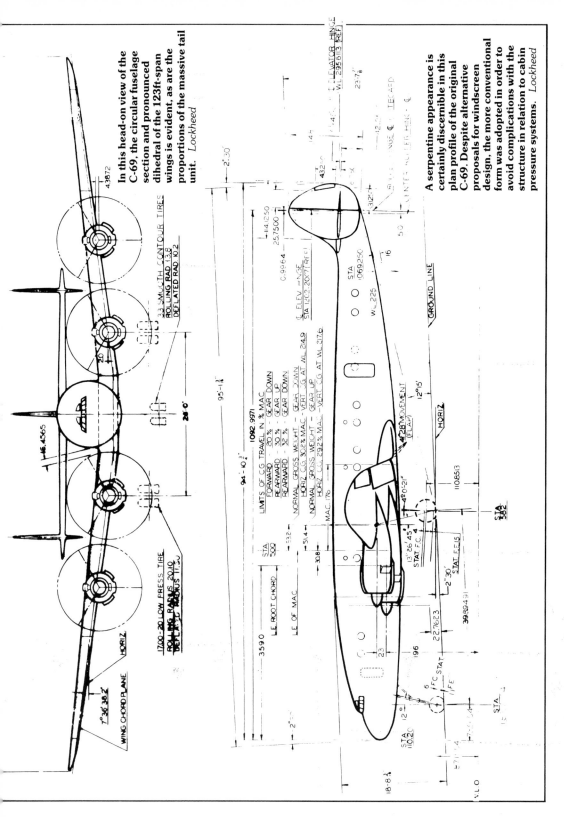

In this head-on view of the C-69, the circular fuselage section and pronounced dihedral of the 123ft-span wings is evident, as are the proportions of the massive tail unit. *Lockheed*

A serpentine appearance is certainly discernible in this plan profile of the original C-69. Despite alternative proposals for windscreen design, the more conventional form was adopted in order to avoid complications with the structure in relation to cabin pressure systems. *Lockheed*

LIMITS OF CG TRAVEL IN % MAC
FORWARD   20% - GEAR DOWN
REARWARD   30% - GEAR UP
REARWARD   32% - GEAR DOWN

NORMAL GROSS WEIGHT - GEAR DOWN - HORIZ CG 302% MAC - VERT CG AT WL 249
NORMAL GROSS WEIGHT - GEAR UP - VERT CG AT WL 2176
HORIZ CG 292% MAC

1700-20 LOW PRESS TIRE
ROLLING RADIUS 2010
DEFLATED RADIUS 1750

33 SMOOTH CONTOUR TIRES
ROLLING RAD 138
DEFLATED RAD 102

WING CHORD PLANE   HORIZ
GROUND LINE

on the nosewheel leg, and in order to reduce this length as much as possible the mean camber line of the fuselage was somewhat lowered at the forward section. A limited downward curve was also incorporated aft of the wing for the purpose of reducing the drag at the maximum lift-drag ratio of the aircraft, thus the fuselage attained a profile roughly similar to the cruising speed airflow over the wing resulting in a small reduction in drag. The fuselage camber line at the rear had also to be raised in conjunction with the horizontal tailplane in order that the triple fins and rudders could be located in accordance with the required ground clearance.

It was initially decided that the flight deck windscreen should be incorporated into the contour shape of the fuselage, but mock-up tests proved this idea to be unsatisfactory, mainly because of poor fields of view and pressurisation problems with that type of structure. Consequently, alternative designs of windscreens were proposed including a faired nose cockpit below the main floor level, twin cupola referred to as the 'bug-eye' type, single wide-type cupola, conventional 'Vee' type and, the

Below:

This Lockheed P-38 Lightning was one of a batch of 667 ordered for the RAF, powered by 1,150hp unsupercharged Allisons. Only three were delivered and the rest of the order cancelled. It was the wing section of this type that was finally adapted for use in the C-69 Constellation. *Lockheed*

type eventually chosen, the single curved conical type.

The design of the flight deck itself provided accommodation for a flight engineer as it was thought the additional weight imposition created by extra controls and instruments was compensated for by the gaining of optimum fuel consumption on long flights. There was also the safety factor to consider whereby an engineer took a certain amount of workload off the pilot, this involving engine checks, cabin supercharging and electrical controls. Also, he was usually more familiar with the aircraft's technical and maintenance background.

Wing design for the Constellation was finalised only after a number of various wing sections had been tested in the NACA 19ft wind tunnel, these including early laminar flow types as well as the more conventional section as employed on Lockheed's P-38 Lightning fighter. It was in fact the P-38 type of wing section which was eventually decided upon for, although there was a drag penalty, this design possessed high maximum lift coefficients and excellent stall characteristics. While the NACA tunnel tests were being carried out it was also an opportunity to test the large chord de-icer boots of the pneumatic-pulse type. Later flight testing, however, proved this type unsatisfactory after a time in service due to disintegration of sections of the boots. This resulted in a thermal de-icing system being developed for the Constellation although it was some years before a

successful combined heating and pulsating system was fitted.

Most major components of the L-49 were tested to destruction at Lockheed's Research Laboratory with a wing joint fracture actually occurring and being corrected. Many parts such as the flaps were subjected to extraordinary life tests under simulated load conditions, while fatigue testing played a prominent part in development of the Constellation's structure.

Because Lockheed had previously built the first pressurised civil aircraft to fly in the USA — the XC-35 Electra — the company was able to draw freely on its experience with that machine in developing a suitable pressure system for the L-49. The result was an initial set of conditions in which cabin pressure, as at ground level, was retained up to an altitude of 9,000ft, while at 20,000ft conditions applying to 8,000ft were maintained. This first system did not include a refrigeration unit although one had been designed for it, while the pressure was maintained by two engine-driven superchargers which could retain full cabin pressure independently.

Based on the findings of the Civil Aeronautics Board (CAB) after several years of investigations into the problem, a high level of fire prevention measures were installed in the engine compartments of the Constellation, the company in addition undertaking a study of electrical equipment installations in relation to fire hazards. To prevent fire spreading from an engine nacelle the entire wing of the Constellation was compartmented to allow proper ventilation, especially around fuel tank areas.

All main components were subjected to vibration tests and any possible flutter manifestation thoroughly checked out. A water ballasting system was also employed in which a central pumping station together with an electric motor pump, large water tanks situated at points along the fuselage and the necessary pipework, enabled engineers to check the aircraft's weight and centre of gravity shift when deliberately altered in flight. To load the cabin with water ballast was a simple operation involving the attachment of a 4in fire hose and manipulation of a valve.

Powerplant tests were rigidly carried out with the fuel system being operated under altitude and varying temperature conditions. To iron out mechanical problems on the ground, a static test-bed was built for the extended running of the Wright engine. Flight testing of the engines was carried out on a Lockheed Ventura, a type with a similar performance to the Constellation, but with two engines. This aircraft, nicknamed 'Ventellation', was later purchased by Curtiss-Wright for further development of the R-3350-35 engines. One test was undertaken to ascertain the minimum time required for a complete engine change on a Constellation and the remarkably fast time of 27½min was clocked.

Left:
High above the swirling clouds in pre-World War 2 days: the sole Lockheed XC-35 (modified Model 10 Electra). Sponsored by the US Army this aircraft (36-353) first flew on 7 May 1937, powered by 550hp Pratt & Whitney turbocharged radials. It was the first 'civil' pressurised machine to fly in the USA and paved the way for pressurisation systems employed in the C-69 Constellation. *MAP*

Below left:
This Lockheed B-34 Ventura bomber — a type evolved from the Lodestar — was employed by Lockheed as a flying test-bed for the Wright R-3350-745C18BA-1 Cyclone 18 radials used to power the Model 49/C-69 Constellation. Unofficially known as the 'Ventellation', this machine later went to Wright's as an engine test-bed. *Lockheed*

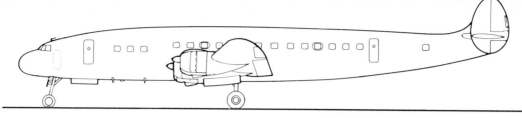

3 Construction, Prototype and C-69

The design and development of the Constellation in its original form covered a period of some four years. During that time, as has been shown, numerous technical problems had to be overcome, but after construction of the first machine was started in 1940 it became increasingly obvious that Lockheed's Model L-49 was probably the most technically advanced transport aeroplane in the world.

The fuselage was an all-metal structure with a circular cross-section, the curved centre-line accentuating the longitudinal aero-foil effect with its lifting qualities. Accommodation was provided for up to 55 passengers with baggage, access to the passenger compartment being by means of a door on the port side of the fuselage aft of the wing trailing-edge. The flight crew entered by a door located forward in the starboard fuselage side and any cargo or large baggage was carried in a freight hold beneath the cabin floor. All cabin space was pressurised to allow for operations up to 30,000ft, while at 10,000ft sea level conditions were maintained.

The wings comprised an all-metal structure of aluminium alloy with a smooth stressed skin and flush-riveted covering; aerofoil sections were virtually scaled-up versions of the Lockheed P-38 Lightning fighter wing aerofoil section. The trailing-edge incorporated the giant area-increasing Lockheed-Fowler type flaps, while alongside were the aluminium alloy ailerons covered by fabric. The wings also contained engine access passages in order that an engineer could attend a troublesome powerplant while airborne.

The empennage, with its large pear-drop shaped triple fins and rudders, was also an all-metal structure with metal-covered fins and horizontal

Below:
Beneath a tropical Pacific sky, the prototype C-69 Constellation (c/n 1961), in its original olive-drab finish, on a test flight over California early in 1943. Initially NX25800, it later became USAAF No 43-10309. *Lockheed*

stabiliser, the rudders and elevators being fabric covered. Trim tabs were incorporated in all these movable components.

A feature of the Constellation was its tricycle undercarriage, the two main units comprising twin wheels mounted on a single Lockheed shock-absorbing strut. They were fully retractable, moving in a forward and upward direction to lie within the inner engine nacelles where folding hinged doors completely enclosed them. The nosewheel with its exceptionally long strut also featured dual wheels, the unit retracting backwards into a recess in the lower front fuselage to be enclosed by a pair of lengthy hinged doors. A retractable skid was installed below the rear fuselage as a precaution in the event of a 'tail low' landing.

The four 2,200hp Wright R-3350-35 Cyclone engines drove a quartet of Hamilton Standard Hydromatic three-blade metal constant-speed fully-feathering propellers. It is interesting to note that in 1943 prior to any official performance figures being released, estimates for the new transport included an operating speed of 280mph at 25,000ft, a landing speed of 77mph and a 4,000-mile range at operating speed. One figure revealed for the military C-69 version after it had entered service was a top speed of 329mph at 16,000ft.

The confidence of both TWA and PAA in the L-49 design was apparent, for even before construction of the prototype started in 1940, TWA had placed an initial order for nine aircraft. This was quickly followed by a contract from PAA for 40 machines of the transoceanic type in June the same year, another 31 also being ordered by TWA at the same time. World events, however, drastically changed the situation and after the Japanese attack on Pearl Harbor which brought the United States into the holocaust of World War 2, the United States Army Air Force (USAAF) decided to invest in the L-49 as a fast military transport. Both TWA and PAA waived their rights to the first batches of production aircraft in favour of the USAAF which ordered 180 Constellations with the military designation C-69.

Towards the end of 1942 the prototype Constellation was ready for taxying and preflight trials for which it was considered necessary to provide the pilot with some form of warning when critical stresses were imposed on the extremely long leg of the nosewheel. These stresses were most likely to occur during rapid turns or with unbalanced application of the wheel brakes or engine power; when such a force manifested itself an indication was passed to the pilot via microswitches attached to the nosewheel struts and a red warning light would glow in the cockpit.

After a number of preflight tests had been undertaken the prototype Model 49, redesignated for military purposes as the C-69, was rolled out for its first flight on 9 January 1943. The aircraft (c/n 1961) carried the civil registration NX25800, but was finished in a military paint scheme of olive drab upper-surfaces and grey under-surfaces. Classified as a USAAF machine it was allotted the military serial number 43-10309. For the initial flight five crew members boarded the prototype C-69, test pilots Milo Burcham (Lockheed) and Edmund T. Allen (on hire from Boeing), research and design engineer Clarence L. 'Kelly' Johnson, with Rudy Thoren and Richard Stanton of Lockheed. As the new transport thundered away from Burbank it was observed by VIPs as well as hundreds of Lockheed employees who cheered the big machine on its way from their vantage points beside the runway or around the air terminal hangars. Even in its drab warpaint the prototype C-69 was a magnificent

Below:
In this view the C-69 prototype has a natural metal finish and is without national insignia, but the USAAF serial has been applied to the fins. Note the retractable tail-skid beneath the rear fuselage.
MAP

sight as the four powerful Cyclone engines bore her elegant shape into the Californian skies for the first time. As a precaution the landing gear was left in the lowered position and, after circling the San Fernando Valley a few times, the new transport headed north to land at the USAAF base at Muroc Dry Lake (now Edwards AFB) after a flight lasting one hour.

That first flight went without incident as did the following five test flights carried out from Muroc Field the same day; the success of these initial flights resulted in almost immediate commencement of the formal test flight programme.

Landings and take-offs were carried out in which failures of the hydraulic booster system were simulated and a number of rough air tests were undertaken in the same conditions. To measure the data on normal landing and take-off behaviour of the C-69, a special grid and timer-camera device was fixed up. This showed the relationship between the wind tunnel and actual flight tests to be a good one. Range tests proved that the prototype Constellation possessed a higher payload factor for its design range than was anticipated and, when flying at a cruising speed of 275mph on 52.5% power, the aircraft used approximately one US gallon of fuel per mile. During exhaustive tests with the C-69 undercarriage layout, one test involved the fitting of small flaps to the tyres which caused the wheels to rotate prior to touchdown. This experiment was found to reduce tyre wear and landing shock appreciably and produced a rotation rate equal to 80% of the actual landing speed. In the case of the main landing wheels the drag on the units was reduced by 30% to that occurring in a landing where no pre-rotation of the wheels was activated. On another occasion one of the cabin windows was deliberately and forcibly removed while the fuselage was fully pressurised and contained a number of personnel. The loss of pressure was found to cause little discomfort to the crew or 'guinea-pig' passengers.

The C-69 prototype was finally handed over to the USAAF for its military acceptance trials at Wright Field, Dayton, Ohio, on 29 July 1943.

The second Constellation to take to the air (c/n 1962) was considered to be the first production C-69 and although intended for USAAF service it emerged in TWA colours. At that time this consisted of an overall polished metal finish with red lettering on the fuselage, red horizontal tail stripes (two on each of the triple fins and rudders), and black letters and numerals on the wings. Despite its civil appearance however, this second Constellation carried the allotted USAAF serial number, 310310 (43-10310), in black digits between the red stripes on the outer fins and rudders.

This particular aeroplane had in fact been prepared for a prearranged nonstop coast-to-coast

promotional flight across the United States by TWA, the two pilots for the trip being Howard Hughes himself and TWA president Jack Frye. Among the flight crew were R. L. Proctor (flight engineer), H. Bolton (navigator) and C. L. Glover (wireless operator); Richard Stanton, R. J. Thoren and Thomas Watkins from Lockheed were also on board. Additionally, a number of VIPs were included as passengers: S. J. Solomon (chairman of the Airline Committee dealing with postwar aviation policies), Lt-Col C. A. Shoup USAAF, and L. J. Chiappino, E. J. Minser, O. R. Olson, L. Sewell, L. Baron, R. L. Loomis and R. de Campo (TWA).

The route chosen covered some 2,400 miles between Burbank and Washington DC, and on the morning of 17 April 1944 at 3.56am the second C-69 roared off into the dawn heading east. Weather conditions for the flight were far from perfect: light icing became a constant problem and caused the aircraft to alter course several times prior to resuming the planned route. The flight was made at altitudes varying between 15,000 and 18,000ft and ended when the aircraft landed at Washington's National Airport after being in the air for 6hr 58min, the first of several records to be made by C-69s in the ensuing years. The Burbank to Washington flight was followed by a week or so of official inspections, special flights and exhibitions designed to impress both military and civilian observers, after which C-69 number 43-10310 was handed over to the USAAF to serve in its intended role as a high-speed transport.

That the US Army had acquired its fast troop transport in the C-69 there was no doubt for, in addition to the excellent fuel consumption figures attained, design performance had been comfortably achieved with a top speed of 347mph and a cruising speed of 275mph. In its commodious fuselage up to 64 armed troops could be transported, or alternatively the aircraft was capable of carrying a light tank or other types of medium sized military vehicles.

On 23 January 1945 TWA's Intercontinental Division was contracted to successfully introduce the C-69 into the USAAF's Air Transport Command (ATC) service, and during this period several significant long distance flights were made. On 4 August 1945 C-69C (42-94550) flew from New York to Paris in a then record time of 14hr 12min. This particular aircraft was the only C-69C model built and was a VIP version fitted out to carry 43 passengers (c/n 1971). After the war this machine was sold on the civil market as NX54212, but although consideration was given to a further 49 of these VIP versions being produced as civil aircraft, no contract ever materialised. Meanwhile on 22 September 1945 another C-69 in USAAF (ATC) service covered the distance of 2,750 miles

between Stephenville, Newfoundland, and Paris in a record time of 9hr 22min.

Altogether 22 C-69s were scheduled for USAAF service when VJ-Day heralded the complete end of World War 2. Including the prototype, 15 had been delivered and a further seven were practically ready for service, these comprising the original nine ex-TWA machines taken over by the USAAF and 13 from the military contract for 180 C-69s signed in 1942. In actual fact the contract was later reduced to a requirement for 73 C-69 strategic transports, but this still left Lockheed with a cancellation order on 51 aircraft. A decision had to be made whether or not to commence design and development of a new version of the Constellation, or convert existing C-69s into a postwar airliner. For five days the Burbank plant was temporarily closed as top level meetings were held by Lockheed executives, and eventually it was agreed to go ahead with a

modification programme to convert the C-69s for civil use and to produce a civil variant proper for airline use. This decision set Lockheed on the road to a great postwar success story and was to secure the company's future in America's aircraft manufacturing industry.

To begin with there was a surplus quantity of Government tooling available, as well as components, constructional material and a number of partially completed C-69s which could be con-

verted into the planned airliner. More important, the jobs of some 15,000 Lockheed employees were reprieved and the company saved so much time that the updated C-69 for the civil market, designated the Model L-049, was 18 months in advance of the Douglas DC-6, Boeing Stratocruiser and Republic Rainbow. Just over a week after VJ-Day Lockheed had a backlog of orders on hand for 103 Constellations for eight airlines with an order book value of $75½ million. After only 27 hours of performance flight testing, the L-049 was awarded the US Civil Aeronautics Board Approved Type Certificate No 763 on 11 December 1945. In the meantime the US War Assets Administration sold off the USAAF Constellations for civilian use, and after modification and refurbishing by Lockheed 19 went into airline service. Two of the military C-69s were destroyed however, one (c/n 1972) 42-94551, in a fire at Topeka on

18 September 1945, the other (c/n 1973) 42-94552, during structural tests at Wright Field. The prototype C-69 NX25800/43-10309, or 'old 1961' as she was sometimes known after the c/n 1961, was later modified to have four Pratt & Whitney R-2800 radials fitted and became the XC-69E. The aircraft was then offered for sale by the US War Assets Administration and purchased by Howard Hughes who appeared to have done little with the machine before he sold it back to Lockheed in 1950.

An intensive modification programme was immediately started on c/n 1961, the most obvious alteration being in the 'stretched' fuselage. This was designed to provide greater payload and a total cabin length of 56ft, these improvements being obtained by the incorporation of two new fuselage sections, 10ft 9in and 7ft 8in respectively, fore and aft of the wing. Power was increased by the

Above left:
This USAAF C-69-5 (c/n 1980), serialled 294559 (42-94559), was one of a number converted to L-049 standard for civil use by Lockheed. It was sold to BOAC as G-AHEN in 1946 and named *Baltimore*. Note the 'Speedpack' freight container beneath the fuselage. *MAP*

Left:
Had it been available 18 months earlier, the Republic RC-2 Rainbow — a 46-seat passenger transport intended for Pan Am — might have been a serious rival to the Constellation, but production status was not reached. This picture shows the Republic XR-12, an experimental four-engined reconnaissance bomber upon which the design of the Rainbow was based. *MAP*

installation of four 2,700hp R-3350-CA1 Cyclones, the porthole style passenger windows were superseded by round-cornered square types, structural strengthening of the airframe was carried out, the pressurisation and air-conditioning was improved to cope with the larger fuselage, cabin heating and cooling facilities were enlarged upon and the fuel tank capacity increased to 6,550 US gal.

Thus did 'old 1961' become transformed into the prototype for the L-1049 Super Constellation, a configuration for which the civil registration was changed from NX25800 to NX67900. In her ensuing career c/n 1961 then flew as a test-bed for the radar developments intended for the WV-2 (US Navy radar picket aircraft) and was fitted with auxiliary fuel tanks on the wing tips. But perhaps this amazing aircraft's most notable achievement was in its use as a test-bed for the 3,250ehp Allison T-56 turboprop engine, one of which was installed in the outer starboard position. The success of this engine's trials on NX67900 resulted in it being chosen as the standard powerplant for the Lockheed C-130 Hercules.

Below:
Looking most resplendent in its Lockheed colour scheme is NX67900, the prototype L-1049 Super Constellation which was in fact c/n 1961, the original C-69 prototype, converted to its new configuration by Lockheed. The aircraft had been 'stretched', new style cabin windows fitted, extra fuel capacity provided and uprated Cyclone 18s installed rated at 2,700hp. The tip tanks, however, were not standard at this stage on civil Constellations. *Lockheed*

Left:
The success of the 3,250ehp Allison T-56 turboprop when installed in the Super Connie prototype — known as 'old 1961' — led to its adoption for the Lockheed C-130 Hercules transport, the second prototype of which is seen here (53-3397) powered by four of the T-56-A-1s. *MAP*

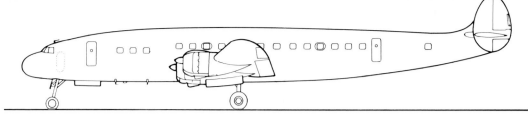

4 The L-049/749 Series

With the exception of the prototype and the two written-off machines, 19 USAAF C-69s became available for the civil market, the majority of these being acquired by TWA and British Overseas Airways Corporation (BOAC). Because of their previous allegiance to the Lockheed Constellation design, TWA were afforded priority delivery of refurbished ex-USAAF Constellations, and also of the newly built L-049 models as they came off the production line ready for civil use. TWA had in fact purchased the last two surplus USAAF C-69s completed at Burbank in December 1945, these being c/ns 2021 and 2022 (ex 42-94560 and 42-94561), which became respectively TWA's N86500 *Star of the Mediterranean* and N86501 *Star of the Persian Gulf*.

The next customer to receive new L-049s was PAA, this company having earlier flown a C-69

(c/n 1963) 43-10311 under USAAF contract. PAA took initial delivery of 29 L-049 models, and on 19 January 1946 one of these flew from New York to Lisbon, Portugal, a distance of 3,425 miles in 9hr 58min at an average speed of 344mph. On 3 February 1946 PAA inaugurated its Constellation

Below:
BOAC acquired a number of Constellations after the war, including this L-049 (G-AHEM) named *Balmoral*. It originated as a USAAF C-69-5 (c/n 1978) serialled 42-94557 and was converted to L-049 standard at Burbank. After its service with BOAC, *Balmoral* was sold in 1955 to Capital Airlines as N2735A (fleet No 755).
via Roger P. Wasley

service between New York and Bermuda, and eight days later the 3,450 miles between New York and Hurn Airport near Bournemouth, Hants (contemporary transatlantic terminal), was covered by another PAA Constellation in 12hr 6min at an average speed of 285mph, this commencing a regular service 'across the pond'.

Meanwhile on 3 December 1945 a TWA L-049 (c/n 2026), N86505, was ceremoniously named *Paris Sky Chief* at Washington's National Airport. This aircraft then left for Paris flying via Gander, Newfoundland, and Shannon, Eire, on an offical proving flight. Unfortunately this machine was lost just over a year later on 28 December 1946 at Rineanna, Eire. On 4 February 1946 TWA's Jack Frye piloted another Connie on a record flight between Burbank and New York, this nonstop effort taking 7hr 28min. The first commercial service

Above:
The graceful lines of a TWA L-049 Constellation adorn the skyline over California. This particular machine (c/n 2024) registered as NC86503, was one of the first civil production aircraft to be delivered to TWA. *Lockheed*

between the USA and France was inaugurated by TWA on 5 February 1946, when L-049 Constellation (c/n 2035) N86511, *Star of Paris*, took off from La Guardia Airport, New York, and headed for Paris. The pilot was Capt Harold F. Blackburn and the flight took just 19hr 46min. Ten days later on 15 February, TWA began its New York to Los Angeles service with Howard Hughes at the controls, the distance on that occasion being covered in 8hr 38min by the L-049.

Left:
The scene is a wet Heathrow in 1946, and the aircraft is Constellation (c/n 2031) N88831 *Clipper London* of Pan Am. It has just landed after becoming the first aircraft on a scheduled transatlantic flight to use the new terminal.
Pan Am

During the early days of its airline service some troubles did occur with the L-049, mainly in connection with engine auxiliary systems, but a setback with more serious consequences took place on 11 July 1946. TWA's N86513 (c/n 2040) *Star of Lisbon* was on a routine company training flight when after some 20 minues in the air the forward part of the aircraft filled with smoke. As a result the crew were unable to carry out an emergency landing and the Constellation crashed at Reading, Pennsylvania, with only one of the six aboard surviving, although he was seriously injured. Investigators found the cause of the fire to have been an electrical short-circuit which had ignited part of the cabin insulation. At the inquiry it was suggested that had an emergency hatch in the passenger compartment been opened, the smoke-

filled area would possibly have cleared. In any event, the crash meant a six-week grounding for Constellations while some 95 modifications and improvements were carried out on the type including electrical systems, fireproofing (this applying to all civil aircraft as an improved standard) and the replacement of the engine fuel injection method by carburettors.

The basic version of the L-049 was technically improved upon through six updates to the L-149, the original L-049 itself, of course, being the 'civilianised' C-69 with a maximum take-off weight of 86,250lb. Next came the L-049A incorporating front wing spar and main landing gear side-strut reinforcements, followed by the L-049B with fuselage detail modifications and new metering pins for the main undercarriage units. Then came the

L-049C featuring a main landing gear strut damper and a 15:1 elevator boost ratio, while the following L-049D had the inner wing sections reinforced. By the time the L-149 appeared with fuel tanks in the outer wing panels, the gross take-off weight had risen to 100,000lb and four 2,200hp Wright R-3350-745C18BA3 Cyclones provided the power.

During May 1945 work started at Lockheed's Burbank plant on a revised version of the Constellation, this being mainly in response to Eastern Air Lines' (EAL) requirement for a medium-range model of the type. By then a 2,500hp version of the Wright Cyclone was available, the R-3350-749C18BD1, and it was this powerplant which was used in the updated Constellation designated the L-649. This variant was in fact recognised as the first truly civil Connie of the postwar era, and on 19 October 1946 the first L-649 (N101A) made its initial flight. Improvements in the design included revised engine cowlings, better air conditioning, more luxurious cabin furnishing and the installation of shock-mounted walling. The new model was designed to carry between 48 and 64 passengers as standard or, for high-density arrangements, 81 seats were made available. There was 434cu ft of cargo space included, extra fuel tanks were installed and the four uprated Cyclones gave the L-649 a cruising speed of some 285mph. An innovation on this version was the 'Speedpack', a special freight pannier which fitted ventrally below the centre fuselage. This pack provided the Connie with an extra 395cu ft of cargo space, enough for up to 8,300lb, and was ideal for use with aircraft on short-haul routes, or where passenger density was low. One airline to so use the Speedpack on its Constellations was Royal Air Maroc.

The L-649 had a gross take-off weight of 94,000lb but this was increased to 98,000lb with the Model L-649A, basically the L-649 with fuselage and inner wing reinforcements as well as modified brakes. EAL purchased 14 L-649As for $650,000 each, and the improvements in air-conditioning and soundproofing turned out to be so good that the type was dubbed the 'Gold Plate Connie'. Entering service with EAL in May 1947 the L-649As began operating the company's New York to Miami, Florida, route the following month.

Meanwhile, even before EAL's L-649As had been delivered, Lockheed's design team were engaged in updating the Constellation layout. This was in response to the international growth of air

Below:
In this excellent shot of Pan Am's L-049 (c/n 2061) N88861 *Clipper Winged Arrow,* **the company has introduced its white upper fuselage scheme as part of the livery.** *Pan Am*

Above:
Improvements to the Constellation resulted in the L-649 of which an interior view is shown here. As well as the more luxurious cabin finish this version had uprated Cyclone engines, and its success earned the L-649 the title 'Gold Plate Connie'.
Lockheed

Centre right:
Looking forward on the compact flight deck of an early L-049 Constellation, in which a flight engineer was employed to ease the workload on the captain and first officer. The throttle quadrant is prominent in the centre of the picture.
Lockheed

Below right:
When compared to the earlier L-049 flight deck, this one installed in the L-749 illustrates a more sophisticated approach. The fuel jettison valves in the roof of the cockpit are particularly noticeable. *Lockheed*

travel in 1947 and the demand by airlines for aircraft with longer range and higher take-off capacity. The revised Connie was designated the L-749 and featured fuel tanks fitted integrally within the outer wing sections. Each of these tanks had a capacity of 565 US gallons which added a further 1,000 miles to the range of the aircraft, thus enabling the 3,660-mile flight between New York and Paris to be made nonstop. The L-749 also featured a strengthened undercarriage and the maximum take-off weight had risen to 102,000lb, but this was not detrimental to the payload which remained the same as the earlier version. Power was still provided by four 2,500hp Wright Cyclone R-3350-BD1 radials, giving a top speed of 350mph and a cruising speed of 328mph. Some L-649s were later modified to L-749 standard. The L-749 was also capable of conveying the underbelly Speedpack as used when required on the L-649, this method of carrying small freight loads in addition to passengers on short- to medium-haul routes proving a great asset. The Speedpack was easily accessible having an electronic hoist fitted for raising and lowering, while any ground handling was facilitated by small wheels inset at each end.

Air France was first in ordering the L-749, the first of 14 machines being delivered on 18 April 1947. In America PAA used the first production L-749 for a record round-the-world flight starting from New York on 17 June 1947. The route taken was via Gander, Shannon, London, Istanbul, Karachi, Calcutta, Bangkok, Shanghai, Tokyo, Manila, Guam, Wake Island, Midway, Honolulu, San Francisco and back across the USA to New York, where the L-749 landed on 1 July.

Early in 1947 an interesting offshoot of the L-749 was projected in Great Britain involving a proposed licence-built version to be produced by the Bristol

Above:

This Lockheed L-749 (c/n 2583) — registered NC91207 and finished in natural metal — was allotted to Trans World Airlines (TWA), and became their fleet No 707 (already applied to the fin in this photograph). *Lockheed*

Aeroplane Co Ltd at Filton, Bristol. This projected Connie was to be powered by four Bristol Centaurus 662 radial engines and it was intended that the type would fulfil a BOAC requirement for a MRE (Medium Range Empire) commercial transport once the aircraft had been suitably anglicised. This plan fell through however, the eventual outcome of the MRE idea ending up in the development of the turboprop-powered Bristol Britannia.

To obtain a higher gross take-off weight and additional payload of 4,850lb, the L-749 design was modified by strengthening the fuselage, inner wing sections and the undercarriage, while at the same time improvements were made to the braking system. The result was the L-749A with a maximum take-off weight of 107,000lb, this version also being capable of conveying the Speedpack ventral cargo pod as fitted to the previous two models.

Air France complemented its original Constellation fleet of L-049 and L-749s by purchasing a further 10 L-749As, while in South Africa four L-749As were ordered by South African Airways (SAA), the first machine, (c/n 2623) ZS-DBR, being delivered on 24 April 1950.

These were the first pressurised airliners to enter service with SAA and they replaced Douglas DC-4s on the Johannesburg to London route, known as Springbok, which flew via Nairobi, Khartoum and

Above:
As depicted in this interior view of a TWA L-749 Constellation, the furnishings were once again improved upon, while outside the cabin more powerful Cyclone 18 engines were installed, outer wing integral fuel tanks fitted and the gross weight increased to 102,000lb. *Lockheed*

Right:
An ex-BOAC L-749A, G-ANTF (c/n 2504), is seen here when flown in the service of Ace Freighters during the mid-1960s. *MAP*

Castel Benito. The Constellations proved far superior in terms of comfort and reduced the journey flying time to 28hr. An interesting, if somewhat tragic, sequel arose three years after the L-749As entered SAA service. With the move to its new International Air Terminal at Jan Smuts Airport (opened 3 October 1953), SAA began introducing jet services with the ill-fated DH Comet I. The Constellations were consequently seconded to operating the Springbok route's tourist class service, the seating arrangements being for 58 passengers. Then followed the tragic Comet disasters at Calcutta, off Elba and Stromboli, with the inevitable withdrawal of Comet Is from airline service. This resulted in SAA reverting to Constellations on its first class service, although the tourist class passengers were still catered for because by then there were five Springbok services operating weekly. The Constellations thus became SAA fleet flagships for the second time, but by 1958 they had been replaced by the Douglas DC-7B, a type which reduced the total flying time for the journey to 20hr. The Constellations continued to operate on SAA domestic routes however, and until January 1959 flew services between Rhodesia (Zimbabwe) and South Africa.

Above:
This early version of the de Havilland Comet jet transport, in the colours of the RCAF Air Transport Command, is representative of the ill-fated type which was responsible for South African Airways L-749A Constellations being initially seconded to tourist class traffic. However, after the tragic Comet disasters which led to the early versions being withdrawn, the SAA Constellations were returned to first class service. *MAP*

Below:
The type which eventually ousted the L-749A Constellations from the SAA Johannesburg to London 'Springbok' service in 1958 was the Douglas DC-7B. Eight hours was knocked off the total flying time for the service, reducing it to 20hr. *McDonnell Douglas*

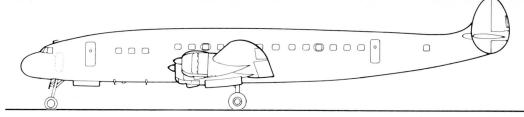

5 The Super Constellation

By the end of the 1940s, despite the fact that a large number of reliable and, on the whole, economical transport aircraft operated with the world's airlines, there was a growing demand for passenger-carrying types which could fly the long-haul routes nonstop. Greatest need was among those companies operating the transatlantic and United States coast-to-coast services, although there was an increasing demand for more advanced types of aircraft on the transpacific routes. Competition was rife among airlines flying the US transcontinental services and a situation arose which led to the two great rival aircraft manufacturers, Douglas and Lockheed, turning to a revision of their already proven designs in the form of the DC-4 and L-749A respectively.

At Burbank the Lockheed team, as previously mentioned, converted the original C-69 prototype (c/n 1961) into a 'stretched' version of the Constellation which, as NX67900, became the prototype for the L-1049 Super Constellation. This aircraft made its initial flight in Super Connie configuration on 13 October 1950, with Lockheed test pilots J. White and R. Meskimen at the controls.

With greater economies and higher payloads in mind, Lockheed's designers had studied the requirements of contemporary airlines very closely indeed. They were especially aware of the potential for a substantial growth in high-density passenger traffic over international long-range routes, factors which would require larger passenger capacity and more powerful engines. Initially the Wright R-3350-956C18CB-1 Cyclone radial rated at 2,700hp was available for the L-1049 Super Connie, while with an extra 18ft 4in of fuselage length, seating was increased to 69 first class, or 92 tourist class. A first class transcontinental sleeper version was available with eight berths and up to 55 first class seats.

The transition from the L-749A to L-1049 Super Constellation was a complex procedure involving more than 550 design alterations of which 360 were maintenance items. Hydraulic pressure was maintained in the Super Connie at 1,700lb/sq in under normal operating conditions, power for this system being provided by four engine-driven Vickers hydraulic pumps. A Bendix hand pump was fitted which gave power in an emergency for the operation of the brakes and undercarriage extension. In addition, separate electrically-driven Pesco hydraulic pumps were installed as individual units for each of the auxiliary rudder and elevator booster systems.

In the design of the landing gear for the Super Constellation, the nosewheel leg of which was 9ft 6in long, hydraulic braking was provided completely in duplicate as a double safety measure, a feature complemented by reverse-pitch propellers where runway length was limited. Another safety angle was the capability of each of the wheels in the twin-wheel units being able to support the full undercarriage strut load when taking off or landing. The nose landing gear was steerable 59° each side of centre and this greatly facilitated the ground-handling qualities for the pilot of a Super Connie.

The wing design for the L-1049 was essentially unchanged, but although aerodynamically the same as the early series, incorporated integrally stiffened skinning on both upper and lower surfaces. This gave a lighter wing structure, reduced production costs and improved fuel tankage within the wings. This updated process was made possible by Lockheed's pioneering attitude to manufacturing techniques in which machines, greater and more

Right:
Although the wings and empennage of the Super Constellation were of identical dimensions to earlier Constellations, the extended fuselage length is noteworthy on this official three-view drawing of the L-1049. *Lockheed*

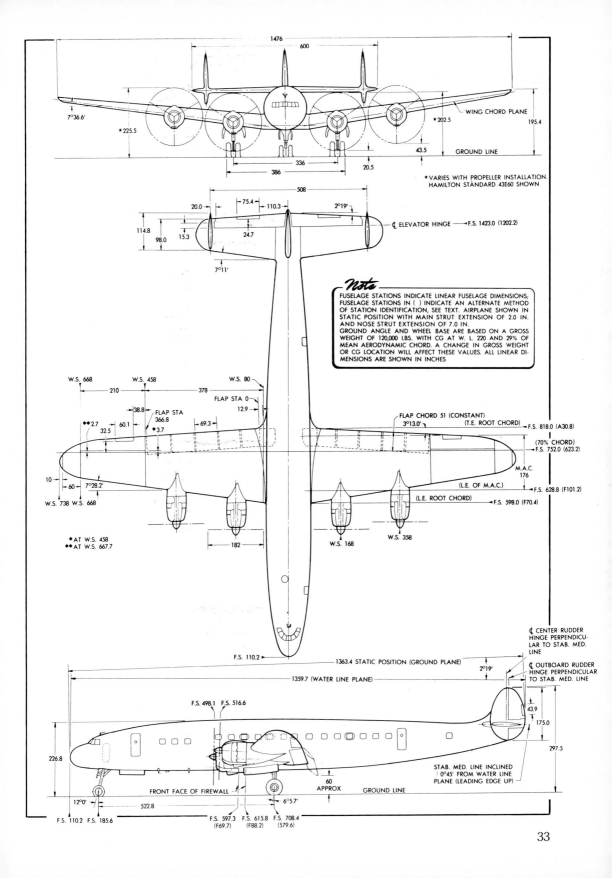

Above:
The flight deck of a Super Constellation, which featured greater headroom than previous models plus improved positioning of controls, red panel-lighting to assist in nocturnal instrument reading, and a laminated, electrically-heated windscreen to aid visibility. Note the auto pilot servo for elevator, rudder and aileron control with its three levers marked *E, R, A* in the lower centre of the picture.
Lockheed

Right:
A proud Australian QANTAS captain poses in front of the Super Connie of which he is taking delivery at Burbank. The 9ft 6in height of the nosewheel gear on a Super Constellation can be appreciated in this picture. *QANTAS*

powerful than any then previously used in aircraft construction, were capable of forming huge pieces of aluminium alloy into the required shape for a specific aircraft component. Thus it was possible to construct massive wing panels of up to 45ft in length in one piece whereby the outer skin and strong inner structure resulted in a single lightweight unit.

This method of aircraft manufacture was carried out in what was known at Lockheed as the Hall of Giants, and the company's employees were confident that their new equipment was symbolic of a new era in aircraft construction technique; it was certainly, as far as Lockheed was concerned, the end of the 'bits and pieces' method. It meant a

3,200lb piece of tough aluminium alloy 32ft long could be milled with great precision until only some 800lb remained. The pieces which had been gouged out were salvageable and in some cases weighed more than Charles Lindbergh's unladen Ryan monoplane *Spirit of St Louis*. The single item for the Constellation which resulted from the machining process proved stronger and lighter than the old types of panel which had required 1,500 separate parts and some 5,000 rivets.

Lockheed's philosophy of avoiding undue weight penalties by taking advantage of previously unused margins of structural strength paid off; it allowed exceptional increases in maximum weight with a minimum of modification. The Constellation airframe could be redesigned with weight reduction as the primary motive, while at the same time modification to the structure resulting in superior strength became a viable proposition. The elongation of the Constellation fuselage was achieved with sound weight economics in mind, the 113ft 7in length of the Super Connie resulting in a payload increase of 40%, while the tare weight (minus fuel, crew and operating service material) was up by only 8,800lb. In the additional cabin space available a further eight standard seats, or 10 tourist class seats,

could be accommodated, thus ensuring airline operators of increased profitability when they used the Super Constellation. Lockheed's sales team worked out a formula for this, emphasising that, given an average flying time per plane per year of 2,930hr, an average cruising speed of 280mph over a distance of 817,000 miles and using the eight standard seats, the annual extra profit would amount to $366,284.80.

In order that Super Constellation passengers would be afforded the utmost comfort and convenience, Lockheed invested $1,500,000 and some 120,000 man-hours in developing and producing what must have assuredly been the most luxurious interior designed for any large capacity passenger aircraft. Priority was given to compartmentation so that considerable privacy could be enjoyed during a flight, while materials used for

Below:
A batch of Super Constellations are pictured under construction at the Lockheed Aircraft Corporation's Burbank complex in the early 1950s. *Lockheed*

furnishings included genuine leather, rich fabrics and natural woods. A club lounge was provided with special lighting effects and restful colour schemes were complemented by artistic murals. Such subtleties of interior decor gave the passenger a sense of security, tranquillity and spaciousness, this latter factor being enhanced by the installation of $16\frac{1}{8} \times 18\frac{1}{8}$in sq (round-cornered) panoramic windows which gave an increase of 85% visibility over earlier porthole-type windows. The new windows had double panes designed to withstand full cabin pressure differential at maximum altitude, these panes being produced from tough non-crazing plastic. They were protected against misting and frosting by means of a circulation of warm air passing between the double safety panes. The windows could also be tinted to obviate high-altitude glare and were installed in such a way that they did not become subjected to any structural load of the fuselage. There was a total of 34 large windows fitted outboard to each row of passenger and relief crew seats, nine of these being mounted in separate emergency exit panels for the use of passengers. Two passenger entrance doors were provided allowing the simultaneous loading and unloading of fare-paying passengers while a separate door gave exclusive entrance and exit for the crew. The interior of the L-1049 also lent itself to flexibility for the airline operator: quick conversion from one class (first) to tourist being possible, for example, or mixed classes could be accommodated.

Like its predecessors the Super Constellation was of course fully pressurised, sea level conditions being maintained at 12,300ft, while when cruising at 20,000ft the cabin pressure was as it would be at 5,000ft, and likewise at an altitude of 25,000ft cabin pressure was equivalent to 8,000ft. Under operating conditions the pressurisation equipment, built and supplied by AiResearch, provided 5.46lb/sq in which was maintained by two engine-driven superchargers, either of which was capable of upholding full cabin pressure on its own.

The Super Connie had what was known as the 'cabin within a cabin' whereby the passenger compartment walling and ceilings were supported within the outer fuselage by isolation-type mountings. Warmed air circulated between the two and even if outside temperatures fell to $-60°F$ the passenger cabin retained a steady 75°F, the units responsible for this being two 125,000BTU/hr internal combustion heaters.

Another equally important requirement for aircraft flying in tropical areas was cabin refrigeration, and on the Super Constellation this was designed to keep the passenger cabin in the 70s when the aircraft was operating in conditions where the outside temperature exceeded 100°F. Individual air outlets were provided for each passenger and on the Super Connie up to 140lb of fresh air could be introduced into the cabin every minute. It was estimated the cooling system on the aircraft was equivalent to running 320 domestic refrigerators which amounted to 16 tons of refrigeration capacity; an interesting comparison when one realises that it requires a ton of refrigeration to freeze one ton of water in 24hr.

In designing the Super Connie, Lockheed's team was aware of the necessity to provide maximum crew comfort and convenience, especially as the type was to operate on both transcontinental and intercontinental nonstop routes. Engine noise level was kept to a minimum and this helped to facilitate communication between crew members considerably as it alleviated the reliance placed upon the intercommunications system. On the transatlantic version a spare berth space was provided for crew members in the forward compartment and, like the passengers, the captain and his crew enjoyed the comforts emitted by the specialised heating and cooling system. Headroom on the flight deck of the L-1049 was greater than on the earlier Constellation series with the controls and indicators located to provide easy access for crew members. Red panel lighting was installed to facilitate instrument readings at night and a system of emergency lighting connected directly to the batteries was available when the aircraft's electrical system was disconnected.

An installation that became standard on the Super Connie was a redesigned laminated and electrically heated windscreen, which gave the captain and flight deck crew some 21% more visibility. This windscreen comprised seven flat panels situated approximately 3½in higher than those fitted on earlier Constellations, and was produced as impact-resistant units mainly as a protection against what is now known as a bird strike. The panels were specially designed to prevent the windscreen from icing over on the outside and misting up on the inside. This was accomplished by applying a layer of transparent conductive coating, known as Nesa, as a heating element. This Nesa (non-electrostatic formulation A) element operated on an input of 1 to 4kW of power, and was sprayed 45 millionths of an inch thick on the inside surface of the outside $\frac{3}{16}$in panel of glass. The centre layer consisted of a $\frac{1}{4}$in panel of elastic vinyl and inside was a $\frac{3}{8}$in panel of glass.

After the troubles experienced earlier with wing de-icers on the first generation Constellations, a new type of improved de-icer boot was developed which would not fragment at speed. These boots which were manufactured by Goodrich operated by means of two pumps which supplied high pressure air to the boots, while two additional pumps were fitted to act as standby or emergency units. Composed from a number of small high pressure tubes, made from a tough weather-resistant synthetic rubber, each de-icer boot unit was built integrally into the leading-edges of the wings, fins and horizontal tailplane. They were in fact as tough as the aircraft's structure itself and formed a smooth, perfectly faired outer profile which extended aft to the 10% chord point on the aerofoils. The boots had no adverse effect on the performance of the L-1049 and by turning on the de-icing system, pilots could free the aircraft of extremely tough accumulations of ice.

A comprehensive electrical system was incorporated in the Super Constellation, a number of machines having as many as six 350A 30V dc generators installed. A new type of generator control system specially developed by Lockheed was also fitted, but produced by the General Electric Co and Hartman Electric Co. This gave protection against over-voltage, under-voltage or feeder faults. The Super Connie also contained an advanced electrical feeder-fault system introduced by Lockheed which virtually eliminated hazards from sparks or electrical faults.

When it came to a choice of propellers for the Super Connie, the airline customer found two types of the three-bladed variety available from Hamilton Standard and Curtiss. The Hamilton Standard type with the 43E60-9 hub and 6903A-0 blades, had fluid anti-icing, hydromatic and hydraulic feathering and reverse pitch. This airscrew was chosen for the Super Constellations which would serve with Eastern Air Lines (EAL), Iberia Lineas Aereas Espanolas, AVIANCA (Aervias Nacionales de Colombia), LAV (Linea Aeropostal Venezolana), Air France, VARIG SA (Empresa de Viacao Aerea Rio Grandense), Braathens SAFE and Northwest Airlines.

The alternative propeller unit from Curtiss was the electric type with a C634S-C502 hub and three 858-C24-0 blades with reversible pitch and fluid anti-icing, or there was the version which had the C634S/C504 hub which differed in having electrically controlled anti-icing. This type was specified for only one airline, Trans Canada, but the version with fluid anti-icing was chosen by KLM, QANTAS, Air India, Seaboard and Western and Pakistan International. Both the Hamilton Standard and Curtiss propellers, as fitted to the Super Constellation, had a diameter of 15ft 2in.

As with the earlier L-649 Constellation, EAL were first in purchasing the L-1049 Super Connie, and on 17 December 1951 the first production aircraft, (c/n 4001) N6201C, went into service on EAL's New York to Miami route. This aircraft had made its initial flight on 14 July that year and was the first of 14 model L-1049s ordered by EAL. Altogether 24 of this basic version of the Super Connie were ordered, the remaining 10 machines going to TWA which introduced the type on their New York to Los Angeles service beginning in September 1952. Those L-1049s used by TWA had additional centre-section tanks, whereas the EAL Super Connies, flying a shorter-haul route, did not require extra fuel.

The basic L-1049 had a gross take-off weight of 120,000lb, and it soon became apparent that, despite the four 2,700hp Cyclones, the type was underpowered if further development was to be considered. But development there was and, strangely, it did not begin with a civil requirement. With the Korean War being fought, the US Navy was in need of a long-range military transport with increased weight, shorter take-off and landing capabilities and, perhaps of most importance, greatly increased power for take-off.

Below:
The advanced concept of the Super Constellation in regard to passenger and crew comfort is exemplified by this L-1049C of Aerlinte Eireann (later Aer Lingus). This aircraft (c/n 4557) registered N1005C, was leased to the Irish airline by the US-based Seaboard and Western Airlines from 1958 until 1960. *Aer Lingus*

6 Turbo-Compounding and the Super Connie

From 1946 onwards the US Navy, as well as other air arms later, employed the Lockheed P-2 Neptune maritime patrol bomber and ASW aircraft. In its P2V-5 (P-2E), P2V-6 (P-2F) and P2V-7 (P-2H) forms this very successful type was powered by two 3,250hp Wright R-3350-30W, and later by 3,500hp R-3350-32W Turbo-Compound radial engines. In the form of Neptune powerplants these engines proved themselves in the saving of fuel and the provision of increased speed, improved take-off and climb performance and range extension. Thus, when the US Navy approached Lockheed with a proposition for a heavier more powerful version of the L-1049 for military use, there was already available for adaptation an engine which had not only accumulated 12,000 hours of experimental testing, but one which was proven during some 160,000 flying hours on the tough rigours of long oceanic patrol.

Although basically the same radial engine as that used on earlier Constellations, the new powerplant chosen for the Super Connie (similar to the Neptune engines) was in fact close to the ultimate in large piston aero-engine design. Rated at 3,250hp

and known as the Wright 972TC18DA-1, this Turbo-Compound (TC) Cyclone was based on the normal Cyclone 18 with additional power provided by three turbines operated through the exhausts from six of the 18 cylinders. The exhaust gases (wasted in a conventional engine) flowed into the ram-air-cooled turbines and were transferred to the propeller shaft via the turbine wheel shaft and the crankshaft. The turbines had no individual control, but some power was provided under any operating conditions, while a fluid coupling gave necessary regulation to the motion so that the turbine was able to take advantage of the exhaust energy without any appreciable increase in back-pressure. The

Below:
The Lockheed P2V-5 Neptune had already proved the reliability of the Wright Turbo-Compound radial engine, when the US Navy requested a more powerful version of the L-1049 Super Constellation from Lockheed. This P2V-5 (128407) is from Navy Squadron VP-26, and is powered by R-3350-30W Turbo-Compounds. *MAP*

turbine wheels rotated with a 6.52:1 ratio over the crankshaft speed, whilst the overall dimensions of the TC engine exceeded those of the ordinary Cyclone 18 by only 11in in length and 2½in in diameter.

The new Turbo-Compound engines contained a number of features designed to give improved longevity of engine working life, with a consequent advantage to potential users through extra profitability resulting from less workshop hours and more hours in the air: the forged steel crankcase eliminated hundreds of studs and their requisite maintenance; the crankshaft itself was short and stiff, therefore being less liable to bend or be subjected to overstressing; the master rods and bearings were made stronger and more durable, and the balanced air distribution, fuel injection and other refinements gave a longer life to the valves, pistons and plugs. The Turbo-Compound's 18 cylinders produced up to 85% of the total power and operated at 43% of power at cruising speed, while there was a 15-20% power increase during the take-off and climb. It was considered that operators would be able to maintain previous fuel

consumption rates, but increase the power by around one-fifth, or alternatively previous power settings could be kept in which case some 20% could be saved on fuel consumption. Passenger comfort itself would also be improved with regard to engine noise: the turbining of exhaust gases was an advantage in this respect as the turbine acted as a miniature muffler, and in any case the TC was less noisy than a conventional piston engine.

With the availability of such an advanced piston engine, Lockheed went ahead with development of the Navy's improved L-1049. This was to be a

cargo/troop transport with an integrally stiffened wing, thus allowing an eventual increase in maximum take-off weight to 133,000lb. Initially known as the L-1049B, this version was given the US Navy designation R7V-1 (later C-121J) and carried a crew of four with up to 106 personnel or alternatively a 14-ton cargo load. It could also operate as an air ambulance carrying 47 stretcher cases with their attendants.

The R7V-1 led to an order from Seaboard and Western Airlines (later Seaboard World Airlines) for a civil cargo version of the L-1049B. It was considered this aircraft would be the answer to the reduction of direct costs in the movement of air freight, the interior being designed to use up every inch of available space in an economical manner. More tonnage could be moved with greater ease than by any contemporary commercial transport, and costwise, freight runs would work out at only five cents per ton-mile.

Weight-saving and money-saving features were incorporated into the all-cargo version including an extruded magnesium floor capable of carrying loads of 1,000lb/lineal ft or 300lb/sq ft giving greater latitude in load placement and arrangement, an electric cargo conveyor and large fore and aft doors for the simultaneous loading and offloading of freight. The conveyor device was recessed into the floor of the aircraft to give maximum unobstructed overhead clearance, and it could move a piece of cargo weighing some 12,000lb at a maximum full load speed of 15ft/min. To facilitate freight handling, small portable snatch blocks or pulleys were fitted into the standard seat fittings thus allowing sideways movement of the cargo. This arrangement was simplicity itself, and loading efforts were limited to sliding the freight items into their appointed positions as they came aboard. Indeed one man was able by this means to load the L-1049B and move the heaviest item of cargo.

In the main cargo compartment there was an availability of floor area amounting to 744sq ft, while in the lower freight compartment 288sq ft was available, the cargo Super Connie therefore possessing 1,032sq ft of floor space which was 29% more than any contemporary commercial type. The floor area itself contained such rigidity that the overall area of the load, not the actual contact area, was the determining factor in floor strength. Tie-down fittings were installed across the floor areas in a grid pattern so that working loads of 2,400lb each in any direction were provided for, with no restriction on the angle of pull. In addition a large centre of gravity travel provision allowed for the widest possible latitude in stowing and unloading freight at intermediate points en route, a factor adding even greater economies in air cargo operations.

The large double door arrangement reduced loading and unloading times to a minimum, the huge rear door (9ft 4½in×6ft 2⅓in) allowing the loading of a freight item 73ft long, 4ft 1in high and 10in wide. The forward door measured 5ft 1½in× 6ft 4¾in.

With all these features it was little wonder that Raymond A. Norden, president of Seaboard and Western Airlines, said of the cargo Super Connie with its 340mph cruising speed, 'The new airplane will lift more tonnage faster and over greater distances than any other commercial aircraft now flying or in production'. Seaboard and Western ordered four L-1049Bs, but this contract was cancelled in favour of four L-1049Ds, a modified Super Connie freighter very similar to the planned L-1049B civil version, but with heavy-duty floor installed and an increased gross take-off weight of 133,000lb as against the L-1049B's 130,000lb. The total cargo volume of the L-1049D was 5,568cu ft, and it could carry a freight load exceeding 36,000lb. The first of these L-1049D Super Connie freighters, registered N6501C, made its initial flight in September 1954 prior to delivery to Seaboard and Western Airlines.

By now Lockheed had an aeroplane that was 84% heavier than when the original L-49 was conceived, 54% heavier in maximum take-off weight than the first production Constellation and which, with Turbo-Compound power, was 48% more powerful. Another asset was the fact that although the L-1049D possessed a gross take-off weight of 133,000lb, the airframe was actually stressed to allow for an all-up weight of 150,000lb.

As the Lockheed model number/suffix implies, the L-1049D actually appeared after the L-1049C, a passenger-carrying version of the Super Constellation in which structural modifications were incorporated to make possible the installation of the Wright 972TC18DA-1 Turbo-Compound powerplants. Lockheed had revised the wing structure to give greater strength as on the cargo version, while the fuselage interior was modified so that although an extra 56lb of internal luxury fittings and added versatility was installed, the actual overall empty weight of the aircraft increased by only 1,584lb. Indeed the modifications to the fuselage interior were such that, in spite of the new Turbo-Compound engines weighing 2,500lb more than the earlier ordinary Cyclone 18s, the fuselage of the L-1049C weighed only 6,279lb against the 7,488lb of the basic L-1049 design.

With a crew of six (including cabin staff) the L-1049C carried up to 99 passengers, and the first of 48 of this version built made its initial flight on 17 February 1953 with Lockheed test pilots J. Fales and C. P. Nicholson at the controls. This aircraft was the first of an order for nine received from KLM (Royal Dutch Airlines), and was registered PH-TFP (later changed to PH-LKP). The following August KLM put this aircraft (c/n 4501) into service on its Amsterdam to New York service, while other airlines which purchased L-1049Cs for their major routes included Air France, EAL, Trans-Canada and TWA.

Fuel tank capacity on the L-1049C was as for the earlier basic L-1049 version amounting to 5,455 Imp gal, but the gross take-off weight was 110,000lb as against the earlier variants' 98,500lb. At an altitude of 23,000ft the L-1049C had a cruising speed of around 330mph and the range, with maximum fuel and no reserves, was 4,820 miles.

With the L-1049C model Lockheed introduced greater luxury for passengers at a time when, with major fare reductions running parallel to declining passenger comforts on world air routes, air travellers were being transported in what to many appeared as winged tunnels. To offset this image Lockheed compartmented the L-1049C to provide an impression of luxury to long-distance passengers. Aft of the flight deck was a crew rest area divided from the first forward passenger cabin by a bulkhead with a door for privacy. Below the front cabin was the forward underfloor freight hold with a 728cu ft capacity. At the rear of this cabin, which seated 12 persons (two rows of six abreast each side of the aisle), were located port and starboard toilet and wardrobe compartments followed by the main passenger cabin at the rear of which was a lounge with seats arranged at various angles. Through the next partition one entered a smaller section in which the galley was located to starboard, while to port was the entry door, lobby, ladder stowage area and a wardrobe. Passing through yet another partition one came to the rear passenger cabin with two-abreast seating, beyond which was a small area for the cabin attendant, a folding seat and port and starboard wardrobes. Aft of this were two washrooms, these being partitioned off from the

two rear toilet compartments situated at the extreme aft end of the cabin area. In KLM's Super Connies the lounge, with its armchair style seating, was extremely comfortable and on the cabin walling, large maps depicted how the Super Connie had shrunk the world with its 330mph cruising speed.

Obviously, with its transoceanic capabilities and luxurious Dreyfuss-styled interior, the L-1049C Super Constellation was a prime choice for nonstop transcontinental services and on 19 October 1953 TWA used the type to inaugurate its nonstop Los Angeles to New York route. This was in direct competition to American Airlines which was employing the Douglas DC-7 series, another transcontinental design similarly powered by Turbo-Compound engines.

As mentioned previously, the L-1049D was an all-cargo version of which four were produced for Seaboard and Western, and this model was followed by the L-1049E. This was similar to the L-1049C but contained modifications which increased the maximum take-off weight to 135,400lb, with a landing weight of 113,000lb. Twenty-six L-1049Es were ordered but a number were converted while still on the assembly line to a further updated model, the L-1049G.

Below:
This serene air-to-air study is of the first of 48 L-1049Cs built and seen here on a test flight from Burbank. The first flight was on 17 February 1953 and this aircraft (c/n 4501) was to be one of nine delivered to KLM. It is pictured in natural metal finish, but carries the Dutch registration PH-TFP (later changed to PH-LKP). This actual machine entered service the following August on KLM's Amsterdam to New York route. *Lockheed*

The L-1049G was in fact basically an L-1049E powered by the uprated Wright 972TC18DA-3 of 3,400hp. This powerplant had become available after Curtiss-Wright had carried out modifications to the original DA-1 design including improved supercharging. Thus with the four DA-3s installed, maximum combined take-off power for the L-1049G amounted to 13,600bhp, while the gross weight increased to 137,500lb; the landing weight remained the same as for the L-1049E and the zero-fuel weight was 108,000lb, although this was initially 104,200lb.

A feature of the L-1049G Super Connie was the provision for optional wingtip fuel tanks to be fitted. These tanks, each with a capacity of 500 Imp gal, had been developed from an idea by design and research engineer Clarence L. 'Kelly' Johnson who originally intended them to give maximum range to a turbo-prop version of the Super Constellation that was planned. However, prior to their adoption for the L-1049G, the tip-tanks were used on US Navy WV-2 early warning radar versions of the Super Constellation. With a total fuel capacity of 6,453 Imp gal (including tip-tanks and optional centre section bag-type tanks) the L-1049G, or Super 'G' as it was often known, was theoretically capable of

a maximum range in ideal conditions at 10,000ft of 4,280 miles. In practise however, taking an example stage length, this figure realistically worked out at 4,020 miles given a headwind of 45mph, reserves for a 230-mile diversion and a possible one hour stand-off at the destination point.

Initially the basic L-1049 model sold for $1.25 million, but by the time the Super 'G' was available the price had risen to over double that amount. Even so the L-1049G proved to be the best seller in the Super Connie range and a total of 104 were produced for the civil market. First user of the Super 'G' was Northwest Airlines (later to become Northwest Orient), the initial delivery being made on 22 January 1955 when (c/n 4572) N5172V was handed over. The type entered service on 15 February when it flew Northwest's Seattle, Anchorage (Alaska), Tokyo, Okinawa and Manila route. TWA placed L-1049Gs into service on their Washington to London route on 1 November 1955, this company having its Super 'G's fitted with weather radar facilities. Other airlines using the Super 'G' followed suit, for although the radar equipment necessitated an extra 3ft in length to the nose of the aircraft, it greatly improved safety and comfort for passengers. The radar informed the crew of adverse weather conditions ahead which were thus avoidable by a course deviation, a factor allowed for in the fitting of the long-range tip-tanks which gave an extra 700 mile range premium.

The L-1049G accommodated between 59 and 63 first class passengers, 47 berths in sleeper configuration or 94 tourist class seats, with a crew of between five and 11 (including cabin staff) depending on whether or not the route flown was interhemisphere.

Below:
This fine view depicts QANTAS Super 'G' Constellation (c/n 4607), VH-EAD *Southern Dawn* with her 3,400hp Turbo-Compound Cyclones in full cry. Note the tip-tanks, kangaroo emblem on outer fins, and Australian flag and name 'Australia' on the central fin. *QANTAS*

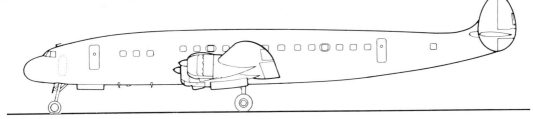

7 Improvements, Turbo-Prop Projects, the L-1049H

With the advent of the Super 'E' and 'G' Constellations, pilots had at their fingertips the means to control some half a ton of advanced electronic equipment installed to aid the crew, with the best in contemporary communications and navigational techniques.

The transoceanic Super Connie was basically fitted out with the following equipment (subject to airline operators' requirements): two HF radio-transmitter/receivers serving 100 channels or more, one VHF set for 20 channels, two automatic direction finders, two visual omni-range (VOR) systems for checking directions from radio ground stations, two glidepath receivers for instrument landings, one marker beacon for checking progress along allotted airways, altimeters, interphones and cabin address systems. With the Super Connie the large earphones, once clamped to the heads of

airline pilots, were phased out to be replaced by overhead loudspeakers. The number of these varied, however, according to the requirements of the airline involved, some aircraft having speakers located at four separate flight stations and up to 12 installed in the passenger compartments.

Improved accessibility and quickly removable electric junction boxes facilitated any required maintenance by the flight deck crew, while externally the Super Constellation was subjected to

Below:
London Airport 1961: L-749A (c/n 2627) CN-CCP of Royal Air Maroc takes on fuel, in this case through the outer port filler well. This aircraft was originally with Air France as F-BAZH. *MAP*

less drag from protuberances by the fitting of low profile antenna.

As already mentioned, all-weather radar based on military equipment was installed on the later Super Connies as it became available; this important addition to the aircraft's safety measures including a scanner which was capable of detecting storms from 50 to 100 miles ahead, and also provided the crew with information on any surface hazards when necessary.

The tankage system on the later models of the Super Connie was similar to that employed earlier on the L-749A version, but modifications included an additional 730 US gal tank which was installed in the unpressurised centre section of the wing. There were seven filler-well openings (one for each tank) located along the top wing surfaces, and these allowed fuel to be added at the rate of 150 US gal/min each. All tanks, with the exception of the new centre section tank, were jettisonable; the outer wing tanks being emptied independently by means of hydraulic jettison valves. The four inner wing tanks could be jettisoned two at a time, with two on one side being emptied at the same time. Fuel from the centre section tank was transferred to the wing tanks before jettisoning. All the fuel tanks were vented by a NACA non-icing, flush, ram vent.

Fuel levels in all seven tanks were indicated on the aircraft's instrument panel by Simmons Pacitron gauges, or alternatively through Liquidometer fuel indicators. On the ground, fuel in each tank was measured by means of a dipstick being inserted through the filler-well, while low level fuel amounts in the outer wing tanks and the outer sections of the inner wing tanks could be measured with an auxiliary dipstick.

There was a distinct advantage in Lockheed's method of incorporating the fuel tanks in the integrally-stiffened wing sections of Super Constellations. Firstly, there were fewer holes to seal, thereby lessening the chance of leaks developing; secondly, increased strength was obtained with the structure and outer skin of one unit; and thirdly, lighter weight fuel tanks resulted, despite the increased strength throughout the section. Another factor in the design of the Super Connie was the structural integrity which would allow the use of turboprop engines with the type when they became available.

With Pratt & Whitney progressing in the development of their T34 axial-flow-type turboprop engine, it had been envisaged for some time that this would be the eventual powerplant chosen to marry up to the Super Constellation airframe. Modifications to the aircraft itself, when the T34 became available, were to include a reduced span resulting from a shortening of the wingtips, increased strengthening of the undercarriage and alterations to the engine control, airscrew control, starting and oil and fuel supply systems. Improvements would also be made to the flight engineer's panels covering instruments and controls, while the cabin supercharger arrangement and its controls would be removed.

If fitted with the turboprop engines, the modified Super Connie would have a 150,000lb maximum take-off weight, with a landing weight of 110,000lb. The structural zero fuel weight (gross weight without fuel) was worked out to be 106,000lb — 6,000lb heavier than the Model L-1049E. The revised transport would also be fitted with wingtip tanks where required, as used on the Super 'G', these giving the proposed L-1249 turboprop version a

Left:
This Lockheed Model L-1249 (US Navy R7V-2) was designed to accommodate four 5,700eshp Pratt & Whitney T34 turboprop engines (YT34-P-12A). With BuAe No 131660 (c/n 4131) it was one of four built of which the Navy retained two, the remaining two being transferred to the USAF as YC-121Fs. The four military machines flew in an experimental capacity only. *MAP*

Right:
Seen at Blackbushe in 1959, L-1049H (c/n 4803) VH-EAN of QANTAS was a passenger/ cargo version of the Super Connie and had a gross take-off weight of 140,000lb. *MAP*

total fuel capacity of 7,750 US gal. Without tip-tanks, the total capacity would be 6,550 US gal, the fuel for the turboprop version being of a low-grade quality similar to kerosene. Work capacity of the L-1249 with turboprop power was expected to be increased from 3,720 ton-mph to 4,760 ton-mph, while the average block speed was estimated to rise from 315mph to 385mph, with a maximum speed of over 425mph envisaged. The competitive life of the aircraft was also expected to be increased by at least four years by the use of turboprop power according to Lockheed's calculations. This whole concept was worked out to a minimum cost formula, based on a transport aircraft that was expected to earn substantial profits before, during and after the introduction of long-range pure jet transports.

From 1954, Lockheed planned to stress all L-1049 models for turboprop power, having already built four such machines for the military, namely the R7V-2 (US Navy) and YC-121F (US Air Force), the latter comprising two Navy machines which were transferred.

Lockheed's ideas centred on two versions of the L-1249: an 'A' model for freighting, and a 'B' model for passenger duties. In both cases they were similar in layout to the L-1049D and 'E' respectively, except for the awaited powerplants and modified undercarriages. There were delays, however, at Pratt & Whitney in development of the PT2F-1, the civil version of the T34 military turboprop engine. At Lockheed, plans and estimates were nevertheless finalised for the L-1249 models and, based on figures obtained for the Navy's R7V-2 version, the results looked very promising. The L-1249A would be capable of a nonstop coast-to-coast flight across the United States in under six hours carrying a 16-ton payload, and at a cruising speed of 440mph. In a similar time it could theoretically fly from Hawaii to California, and in an estimated 8hr 45min make the New York to London transatlantic run (via Gander). With its gross take-off weight of 150,000lb the L-1249A would have a service ceiling of 35,800ft, the 8,750gal fuel load being contained in the normal wing tanks, wingtip tanks and in underwing tanks, the tip tanks holding 600gal apiece. The absolute range was estimated as 4,150 miles and the type was expected to have a cruising speed of 368mph at 25,000ft. Other factors worked out in connection with the proposed L-1249B model gave a sea level take-off at gross weight in which a 50ft high obstacle would be cleared in a take-off run of 2,900ft. On landing (110,000lb) after clearing a similar projection, the aircraft could carry out its landing run and stop in a distance of 3,500ft. At a weight of 110,000lb the L-1249B would fly at an average block speed of 385mph on a 2,500-mile flight. Estimated top speed in this form was 411mph.

Despite the potential of the turboprop Super Constellation no civil orders were forthcoming, but Lockheed went ahead with two further projects in which not only the Pratt & Whitney PT2F-1s were considered, but also the British Rolls-Royce RB109, which would become known as the Tyne. The first project involved a model termed the L-1449 in which a new wing design was formulated. This consisted of a laminar-flow layout in which the span was increased to 150ft. The fuel tanks were still integral with the wing structure, but the capacity had increased to 9,600 US gal. In addition the fuselage was lengthened by 4½ft but the gross weight was still 150,000lb, while the payload worked out at 16,460lb. The estimated cruising

speed for the L-1449 was put at 430mph, with a maximum range of well over 5,000 miles.

This model was further improved upon by the planning of an even more advanced project, still designed for the turboprop engines, but with a fuselage in which the length was increased by almost 11ft. This version was known as the L-1549, and the gross take-off weight was to be 187,500lb, the payload being some 18,000lb. This aircraft would have a range exceeding 4,000 miles and had an estimated cruising speed of 410mph at 30,000ft.

In the event, with further delays in the PT2F-1 turboprop programme resulting in uncertainty about the engine's availability, Lockheed decided to drop their turboprop Super Constellation ideas. Consequently the L-1249 programme was cancelled and the L-1449 and L-1549 projects abandoned. However, the whole concept was not wasted, for from this set of projects Lockheed was able to use a number of ideas, especially the revised wing, in a forthcoming venture known as the L-1649 Starliner.

Meanwhile, at Burbank, a hard look had been taken at the possibility of a multi-purpose version of the Super Constellation. It was thought of as an already proven airline type which would be capable of conveying either passengers or cargo by means of a rapid conversion technique and would appeal to operators as an economical proposition.

The idea was put into practice and on 20 September 1956 the prototype L-1049H made its initial flight. This aircraft, c/n 4801 (later sold to QANTAS of Australia as VH-EAM), powered by four 3,400hp Curtiss-Wright R-3350-972-TC-18 EA-6 Turbo-Compound engines had a gross take-off weight of 140,000lb, and was the first of 53 L-1049H Super Constellations built.

The fuselage of this variant had been re-stressed and strengthened so that it was capable of carrying around 20 tons of freight, a maximum payload of 38,000lb being possible on North Atlantic nonstop city-to-city routes. Basically the L-1049H was a convertible version of the L-1049G fitted with the specialised freighter equipment incorporated in the earlier L-1049D cargo variant; conversion to passenger carrying configuration could be quickly carried out by the addition of toilets, interior lining panels, cabin luggage/baggage facilities in the form of racks, seats for up to a maximum of 109 passengers (tourist class), a buffet/bar and other passenger requirements. The L-1049H was fitted with the 'D' type heavy duty cargo floor, and retained the fore and aft cargo doors of the 'D'. The main freight compartment measured 1,883ft in length and could hold 593cu ft of bulk loads or individual items of cargo. Below the main cargo space there was a second freight hold.

The 53 L-1049Hs produced were delivered to a number of airlines including the famous Flying Tiger Air Lines, an all-freight concern, the last Super Constellation built, L-1049H (c/n 4835) registered N6925C, fleet No 815, being delivered to that airline in November 1958.

By December 1959 Flying Tiger Air Lines had acquired a fleet of 14 L-1049Hs, this number rising to 21 machines by 1962. This airline certainly received its value for money from the Super Connie 'H' model, for its aircraft were often working 12 hours per day schedules with an 84% load factor!

A main user of both the Connie and Super Connie was TWA which also put a number of L-1094Hs into service, and indeed it was TWA which carried a record weight of mail on an overseas flight on 13 December 1957. The Super 'H' was on that occasion fitted out as a special mailplane for the purpose of conveying a maximum load of Christmas mail to United States military personnel stationed in Germany. On that pre-Christmas flight across the Atlantic, 61,000lb of parcels, letters and cards were delivered, of which some 23,000lb went to US Forces in and around Frankfurt alone.

Prior to the emergence of the L-1649A Starliner, the L-1049H was considered the ultimate in long-range transport aircraft in comparison to contemporary types. However, it was acknowledged that some of the later orders for the 'H' model were based on it being employed only as an interim type for passenger work; the main factor in the L-1049H's favour was its resaleable value as a pure freighter aircraft.

Right:
Seen at Miami International Airport in 1978, this L-1049H (c/n 4820) N-1880 is nearing the end of its days. It had enjoyed a very chequered career having operated with Lufthansa, Slick Airways, South Pacific Airlines, Alaska Airlines (leased to Airlift International), Conner FA, Montreal Air Services Ltd (leased to World Wide Airways) and Nordair. *Roger P. Wasley*

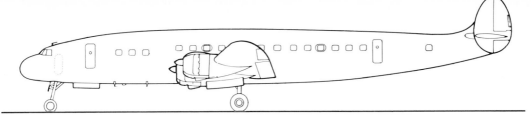

8 Military Constellations

As mentioned earlier, the end of World War 2 saw the USAAF cancel its Lockheed C-69 Constellation contracts. This was just after VJ-Day (15 August 1945) and at that time 21 C-69s had either been delivered or were nearing completion for military service. These included eight C-69-1, 10 C-69-5 and two C-69-10 63-seat troop carriers, while one aircraft, designated C-69C (later ZC-69Z) was produced as a 43-seat VIP transport. Among variants of the military Constellation cancelled were 49 C-69C VIP high-speed command transports with a 43-seat capacity, a number of C-69As having accommodation for 100 troops, several C-69Bs with seating for 94, and three C-69Ds built to carry 57 personnel, all these C-69 models being designed to carry a crew of six.

After the war Lockheed was busily engaged in its civil Constellation programme, and it was three years before any further military interest was shown in the developing Connie design. In 1948, the United States Air Force (USAF) was attracted by the long-range version of the L-749 — the L-749A — and decided to place an order for 10 machines intended as long-range military personnel and freighter transports. Designated as C-121As (Lockheed Model 749A-79-38) these new military Connies were powered by four 2,500hp Wright R-3350-75 radials, and had heavy-duty flooring installed for cargo shipment, while a rear fuselage freight door facilitated loading and offloading of cargo. Alternatively seats, removable as required, could be fitted for the personnel-carrying conversion, or the aircraft could be used as an ambulance with the provision of hospital stretchers.

Three of the C-121As were converted as VIP transports to be designated VC-121As, one machine (48-613) being used by Gen MacArthur and named *Bataan*, a second (48-614) named *Columbine I* and the third (48-610) Gen Eisenhower's own *Columbine II*. As Eisenhower's personal aircraft, *Columbine II* had a very chequered career worthy of note. It received the nickname 'Gen Ike's Eagle', and with the General as NATO Commander at that time, was stationed in Paris from where it flew to most of the major Allied bases and airports in Europe. Quite a number of transatlantic flights were also made, and the

Below:
The USAF version of the Constellation after the war was the C-121A (Lockheed Model 749A-79-38) of which nine were built. Seen above a mountainous landscape, this particular aircraft (c/n 2604) 48-612, is in MATS service, the engines being 2,500hp R-3350-75s. *Lockheed*

Far from land above the watery wastes of the ocean a US Navy WV-2 (EC-121K in 1962) is on patrol. Based on the L-1049B, the type carried a crew of 26 and could remain airborne on oceanic patrols for up to 30hr. *Lockheed*

specially chosen crew of eight led by the pilot, Maj W. G. Draper, clocked up some 50hr a month in the air.

After being replaced in 1950 by a VC-121E, *Columbine II* operated as a VIP transport out of Washington DC until 1954, when it returned to Europe for the use of Gen Gunther. After another spell of VIP duty back in Washington, 48-610 was finally declared redundant as far as the USAF was concerned. The aircraft was then purchased by TWA before going to Ethiopian Airlines as ET-T-35, in which service it was the personal aircraft of Haile Selassie, Emperor of Ethiopia, in 1957. In fact it was in that year that this particular Connie met her end: on 10 June, while flying near Khartoum, one of the engines caught fire and the machine made a forced landing. All on board escaped, but Constellation c/n 2602 was burnt out.

In addition to the C-121As built, a one-off machine was produced designated the VC-121B, this being a staff transport fitted out with a VIP interior, and equipped for possible use by the US President. It carried the USAF serial 48-608 (c/n 2600) and was named *Dewdrop*. A further six VC-121Bs were put into service but these were all conversions, three C-121As (48-611/612/617) and three VC-121As, those described above.

Remaining C-121As in service flew with the USAF Military Air Transport Service (MATS) and at one time were temporarily reclassified as PC-121As.

During the 1948-49 Berlin Airlift, C-121As of the MATS played an important part in helping convey personnel and essential supplies of food, fuel and other commodities to Tempelhof aerodrome in Berlin. Indeed the first month of the Russian blockade saw the military Constellations clocking over 5 million miles as they flew a shuttle service of supplies across the North Atlantic from the United States to Germany.

During the same period developments in radar were making rapid progress and the US Navy decided the Lockheed L-749A long-range Constellation would make an ideal platform from which to try out the latest early warning radar and intelligence-gathering electronic equipment. Consequently two such aircraft were ordered from Burbank initially designated PO-1W (later WV-1), the first machine c/n 2612 (BuAer No 124437) making its initial flight in June 1949. Soon nicknamed 'Po Ones', these two Airborne Early Warning (AEW) pickets proved quite successful. They had extremely large radomes fitted above and below the fuselage, the upper protuberance having the appearance of a nuclear submarine's conning tower, while along the top of the fuselage were erected a number of antennae. These radomes and their complementary equipment, with height-finding radar in the top dome and plan surveillance radar in the lower teardrop-shaped one, were designed to seek out enemy aircraft and surface ships respectively in time of war. A crew of 22 was carried involving aircrew, radar operators and engineers, and with their extensive range both in duration and amount of electronic equipment, the PO-1W (WV-1) concept was to become an accepted and essential part of naval strategy. As for the two PO-1Ws, apart from interior alterations, the only external modifications required to compensate for the extra area taken up by the radomes was an increase in dimensions of the fins.

The US Navy's faith in the Constellation design had already been proved. Initially a naval transport version of the L-049 was ordered designated the R70 (Model 049-46) and although no BuAer numbers were allotted, this type served with Navy Squadron VPB-101. With the advent of the L-1049 Super Constellation, the Navy had invested in the R7V-1, a cargo/troop carrying version with a redesigned wing structure, heavy-duty floor, forward and rear cargo doors and powered by four 3,250hp Wright R-3350-91 Turbo-Compound engines. Now, with the favourable results from the AEW PO-1Ws to work on, the Navy placed a production order with Lockheed for a number of flying radar stations based on the R7V-1 layout one of which, designated as a R7V-1P, was to be fitted out with photographic equipment and fly on reconnaissance sorties over the Antarctic region. The R7V-1 was also modified to carry weather-warning radar, this being installed forward of the flight deck and necessitating an extra 3ft of nose length.

After the end of World War 2 the idea of flying radar pickets, which were really airborne electronic sentries capable of extending the range of surface-type radar by great distances, was put into practice by the United States using World War 2-type bombers. Twenty-three Boeing B-17Gs (ex-USAAF) were converted for the Navy by having extra fuel tanks installed and a large radar scanner fitted into the bomb bay. These aircraft, designated PB-1W, also had their defensive armament removed when the APS-20 search radar was installed. Two B-29 Superfortresses were also transferred to the US Navy as P2B-1 radar pickets, these too having additional fuel capacity and search radar installed in the bomb bays. Then came the

Right:

Life seems to be a bed of roses for this US Navy R7V-1 (c/n 4136) as it refuels in 1963. Operating out of the NAS at Keflavik, Iceland, this machine (BuAe No 131635) represents the Navy equivalent of the Lockheed L-1049B Super Constellation design, with revised wing structure, heavy-duty flooring, front and rear cargo doors and the 3,250hp Wright Turbo-Compound Cyclone engines. *MAP*

Below right:

Progenitors of the US Navy's flying radar pickets, and hence of the Lockheed WV-2 Warning Stars, were a number of World War 2 Boeing B-17G Flying Fortresses transferred to the US Navy as PB-1Ws. This example (c/n 32515) was USAAF 44-83874, but is here seen in its PB-1W form as BuAe No 77237. Note the 'guppy' radome located in the belly of the aircraft. *MAP*

Lockheed PO-1W trials which paved the way for the most diverse series of military types based on the Turbo-Compound-powered Super Connie which, after the 1962 US Forces redesignation system, carried the EC-121 suffixes to letter T.

Entering service during the mid-1950s, the new AEW Super Constellations for the US Navy were initially designated as PO-2Ws, later amended to WV-2 (EC-121K in 1962), and were officially given the name 'Warning Star'. Power was provided by four uprated 3,400hp Wright R-3350-34 or 42 Turbo-Compound Cyclone 18s, and wingtip tanks were fitted similar to those on the civil Super 'G' to allow maximum possible range, the result being a flight duration of up to 30hr. A crew of 26 was carried, the radar operators sitting to face consoles and radarscopes which involved nearly 6 tons of radar, electronics, data links and communication systems used in AEW operations. Provision was made aboard the ocean-going AEW aircraft for some of the crew to take a spell off duty, bunks being part of the furnishings, although the radar and its complementary equipment took up about half of the cabin space. A galley was installed nevertheless, enabling the off-duty crew to take advantage of the facilities for preparing a hot meal and drinks. Also each WV-2/EC-121K carried a good supply of spare components in order that any necessary

Above:
This Lockheed WV-2E (c/n 4301) (which became EC-121L in 1962) is BuAe No 126512 and is equipped with AN/APS-82 aerial surveillance radar contained in the large rotating dish weighing 9 tons. The first flight was in 1956, but this version of the Navy's Super Connie did not reach production status. *Lockheed*

running repairs could be undertaken while the aircraft was still on patrol.

A number of WV-2s were converted to become WV-2Qs, these being fitted out with sophisticated electronic countermeasures (ECM) equipment, direction finding (D/F), jamming devices and additional aerials and antenna aft. In 1962, the WV-2Qs were, in accordance with the revised classification system, redesignated as EC-121Ms.

One WV-2, designated as a WV-2E (later EC-121L) and carrying BuAer number 126512 (c/n 4301), was chosen to be equipped with a new aerial surveillance radar known as AN/APS-82. This was contained in a large rotating dish weighing 9 tons which was mounted on top of a massive pylon incorporated into the aircraft's upper fuselage. This combination made its first flight in

1956, but the EC-121L did not reach production status although the Grumman WF-2 Tracer, using a rotodome dish scanner, was accepted by the US Navy for carrier use.

A special weather reconnaissance version of the Super Connie was also supplied to the US Navy designated the WV-3 (later WC-121N), eight of these being built with BuAer numbers 137891-137898 (c/n 4378-4385), while one WV-2, BuAer number 141323 (c/n 4447), was converted to WV-3 configuration. Two machines, BuAer numbers 137895 (c/n 4382) and 137898, last of the above eight built, were later transferred to the USAF becoming EC-121Rs 67-21471 and 67-21472 respectively.

Although using the same basic airframe as the WV-2 as well as having the large radome and ventral 'guppy' dome, the WV-3 weather planes contained a different layout in which the plotting crew was reduced to eight, while the wingtip fuel tanks were deleted. These nine weather reconnaissance aircraft earned for themselves the nicknames 'Storm Seeker' and 'Hurricane Hunter', the type of radar they used being capable of covering over 190,000sq miles of ocean in one sweep. Operating with Navy Squadron VW-4, the weather-seeking Super Constellations flew from the US Naval Air Station at Roosevelt Roads, Puerto Rico, and from Jacksonville in Florida.

The US Navy became interested in another Lockheed proposal for the Super Constellation involving the fitting of turbo-prop engines. During 1952 the decision was taken to produce a Super

Connie powered by four 5,500ehp Pratt & Whitney YT34-P-12A turbo-prop engines driving Hamilton Standard Turbo Hydromatic propellers, 15ft in diameter and having paddle-type blades, each 2ft in width. The US Navy placed an order for four such aircraft in the knowledge that, at that time, the R7V-2 as it was to be designated, would emerge as perhaps the world's fastest propeller-driven transport aircraft. The first R7V-2 made its initial flight on 1 September 1954 and by the summer of 1955 all four aircraft were flying.

Wingtip tanks were featured on the R7V-2s, each containing 600 US gal which gave the aircraft a total fuel capacity of 8,750 US gal. The maximum take-off weight allowed for was 150,000lb, while the service ceiling was 35,800ft. At full power for take-off the Pratt & Whitney T34s were running at 11,000rpm, but the huge propellers, due to a very efficient gear-reduction arrangement, rotated at only 1,000rpm.

It was considered the R7V-2s were a viable proposition and had great military and commercial potential, but it was not to be. There was little interest shown in the type and no production orders were forthcoming, the four R7V-2s built remaining virtually as test aircraft. Initially they were allotted BuAer numbers 131630-131631 (c/n 4131-4132) and 131660-131661 (c/n 4161-4162), but in 1956 the latter two machines were transferred to the USAF as YC-121Fs serialled 53-8157 and 53-8158 respectively. One of the two remaining US Navy machines was later flown as a test-bed with four 3,750ehp Allison 501-D13 turbo-prop engines and nacelles as used on Lockheed's Model L-188 Electra airliner.

Two other Navy variants were the NC-121K, converted EC-121Ks for special purpose tests and projects including 'Birdseye', the ASWEPS programme and 'Magnet' in which the earth's magnetic field was studied and mapped out, and EC-121Ps, another batch of EC-121K conversions equipped for anti-submarine warfare (ASW), their interiors

being fitted out with ASW sensors and Navaids for operations over water. In addition a substantial number of US Navy R7V-1 (later C-121J) transports were transferred to the USAF, which was another major operator of the military Super Constellation.

Following the success of the C-121A the USAF ordered the L-1049 Super Constellation in 1951, designating it the C-121C for long-range transport duties, 75 personnel, 14 tons of freight or 47 stretcher cases being carried as dictated by circumstances.

The C-121C, powered by four 3,500hp Wright R-3350-34 Turbo-Compound radials, grossed 135,400lb take-off weight, an increase of 28,400lb over the earlier C-121A model. The USAF, like the Navy, realised the Super Connie was an ideal aircraft for the AEW role and 10 machines designated the RC-121C were initially ordered. These Air Force flying radar pickets were loaded with some 15,000lb of radar equipment including ANAPS-20 search radar and APS-42 cloud collision gear. The aircraft was similar in profile to the Navy WV-2 in having the upper and lower radome layout, the 8ft vertical dome above the fuselage housing the height-finding antenna, while the lower 'guppy' ventral dome contained the bearing scanner. No wingtip tanks were fitted to the RC-121C, but with a maximum load the endurance at a cruising speed of 335mph was 24hr given reasonable weather conditions. These RC-121Cs (redesignated EC-121C in 1962) entered service with the USAF Air Defense Command in 1953, and were used mainly to patrol the western seaboard of the United States.

During May 1954, the first of 72 updated machines were delivered to the Air Force designated the RC-121D Warning Star (later EC-121D). These aircraft featured wingtip auxiliary fuel tanks, a consequent longer operating range and had improved AEW equipment and electronics. They operated as long-range patrol aircraft and as a flying control centre for the guidance of interceptor

fighters, being known as AEW&C (Airborne Early Warning & Control) aircraft. This variant also provided the basis for several other types of advanced electronics/surveillance machines, the total gross weight for take-off now having risen to 143,600lb.

In 1962, with the designation to EC-121D, a computer and other updated electronic equipment was added to the aircraft in order that it could operate together with other forces committed to the defence of North America under the NORAD/SAGE (North American Air Defence/Semi-Automatic Ground Environment) programme. Further developments in radar and electronics technique led to 42 EC-121Ds being considerably modified internally by having SAGE data-links, a larger airborne computer, revised navaids and other updated electronic equipment installed. Designated the EC-121H this version was distinguishable by the extra radome, a small streamlined affair, located atop the fuselage a little way ahead of the main large radome. Most of these AEW&C aircraft operated with the USAF (ADC) 551st Airborne Early Warning & Control Wing, which was based in Massachusetts at Otis Air Force Base (AFB), and in their more sophisticated form, fed information to NORAD surface bases. However, a number of machines were temporarily converted as radar crew trainers with the designation TC-121C, but these aircraft later reverted to their EC-121C configuration. Two EC-121Ds serialled 52-3416 (c/n 4334) and 55-137 (c/n 4410) were equipped with special classified electronics and designated as EC-121Js.

Another operator of the Warning Star was the 552nd AEW&C Wing of the USAF based at Sacramento, California, and it was this unit which took delivery of four EC-121Q aircraft, EC-121Ds specially adapted for the AWACS (Airborne Warning & Control System) role.

In Vietnam three types of ground sensors to relay information back to American forces were employed — two which buried themselves in the ground leaving just the antenna above the surface, and one attached to a parachute intended to hang from trees. These sensors were dropped from either fast low-flying jets or slow twin-engined aircraft, and the intelligence signals they sent out were picked up by specially modified EC-121K/EC-121P Super Connies converted from USAF use. These operations were known as Project 'Igloo White' and the modified Super Connie relay stations, of which 30 were supplied, designated EC-121R. They did not have upper or lower radomes, but featured wingtip tanks and were in a tactical camouflage finish.

EC-121Rs were chosen for Project 'Igloo White' mainly because of their ability to fly low-level missions for up to 20hr if necessary, while maintaining an accurate course which kept them within receiving range of the signals being emitted by the ground sensors. The information received from these sensors was relayed by the EC-121R crew to an Infiltration Surveillance Centre (ISC) in Thailand. Sometimes, where delays might occur in relation to ISC processing when a vital target was involved, the EC-121R was able to send the required information direct to attack aircraft already airborne.

Over 220 of the main types of AEW Super Constellations were supplied to the US Navy and Air Force, many during their lifetime having the interior completely re-equipped with updated electronics, while other machines underwent a programme of rebuilding. Some of the less electronically sophisticated models continued to operate with the Air Defence Command into the 1970s however, and a number of machines served with the 79th Air Reserve Squadron (915th AEW&C G), which operated out of Homestead AFB, Florida, on Atlantic patrol duties. Aircraft used by this unit in the late 1970s included the EC-121T, an update of the EC-121D for use as an Elint electronic intelligence platform in which a computerised AEW&C feedback system was installed. In this variant the large dorsal radome and its relevant equipment was deleted, while beneath the forward fuselage a cooling air intake had been incorporated. The EC-121T was in fact the heaviest of the Super Constellation range having a gross take-off weight of 152,500lb; at least 24 of these machines are believed to have been delivered. EC-121Ts were the last of the Warning Star series, some aircraft being deployed from the Iceland base at Keflavik until 1978. A few EC-121Ts did retain their large radomes, and it was one of these, 54-2307 (c/n 4389), which had the distinction of being one of the last Warning Stars in service.

In its pure transport role, the military Super Connie served not only with the US Navy and Air Force, but with the Air National Guard (ANG) in its C-121C and C-121G versions, one of the type's primary roles being that of aeromedical evacuation. One Navy EC-121M serialled 135756 (c/n 4323) was flown by the US Navy Pacific Missile Range Squadron in a special colour scheme comprising white upper fuselage and radome, orange/red (day-glo) front fuselage, tail unit (rudders black) and rear fuselage, black nose cone, with the rest of the aircraft in US Navy blue finish and the word NAVY in white lettering on the fuselage sides and beneath the port wing. Another Navy Super Connie, BuAer number 131642 (c/n 4143), later C-121G (54-4065) in USAF, was leased to National Aeronautics & Space Administration (NASA) for use by the Goddard Space Flight Centre. This was in connection with the evaluation of tracking equipment involving the Mercury, Gemini and Agena projects and flights. From May to October 1966 this aircraft was stationed in Australia, later returning to the USA. Originally allotted the registration NASA20, this Super Constellation became NASA420, but later transferred to the US Army for use at a Maryland proving ground.

The Indian Air Force (IAF) also operated the Super Constellation, nine L-1049 Super 'G' types being acquired from Air India, eight for the maritime reconnaissance (MR) role and one as a transport. The reconnaissance machines flew with No 6 (MR) Squadron of the IAF, but although able to undertake long distance patrol duties, they could only provide limited information on the movement of surface ships. They came under the control of the Maritime Air Operations Directorate, a 1971 organisation also capable of calling on attack aircraft for any necessary interdiction duties.

At a sale of surplus US military aircraft in November 1983, four C-121Cs and nine EC-121Ts were offered. Only one EC-121T was sold, and with bidding too low, the remaining 12 ex-military Super Connies were destined to end up as spares or scrap.

Above right:
The Air National Guard Bureau (AFANG) operated this Lockheed C-121C (c/n 4200) serialled 54,0181, in 1973. The type's primary role in the ANG was aeromedical evacuation. *MAP*

Right:
Lockheed EC-121S Warning Star (c/n 4174) serialled 54-155, stands at Lackland AFB. The EC-121S was an updated C-121C converted to EC-121Q standard.
Roger P. Wasley

Left:

Mildenhall, England, 26 August 1978: in the foreground is Lockheed EC-121T (c/n 4389) serialled 54-2307 of the USAF (AFRES) 79th Airborne Early Warning and Control Squadron. This aircraft, on a visit from its Homestead, Florida, base, was one of the last Warning Stars in service and also one of the few EC-121Ts which retained its dorsal radome. *Roger P. Wasley*

Below left:

As on a number of EC-121Ts, the dorsal radome has been deleted on this USAF (AFRES) machine (c/n 4332) serialled 53-3414, seen on a visit to Mildenhall. *Roger P. Wasley*

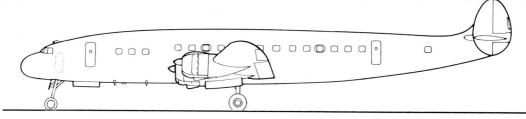

9 Starliner — the Ultimate Constellation

The story of the Super Constellation's development programme was really a battle of the giants. With the introduction of the L-1049C by Lockheed, the Douglas Aircraft Co responded with their DC-7 built at the request of American Airlines who saw TWA's Super Connies as a threat to their own transcontinental traffic. Subsequent developments at Douglas then produced the DC-7C 'Seven Seas' which, with an increased wing span and additional tankage, was capable of undertaking nonstop transatlantic flights in both directions. This aeroplane was a success story for Douglas, and Pan Am was first among a number of airlines to put it into service on 1 June 1956.

TWA responded with a request to Lockheed for an updated Super Constellation which would be competitive with the DC-7C. The result was the L-1649A Starliner, a much larger and more sophisticated variant than its immediate predecessor the Super 'G'. The Starliner was in fact the four-engined piston airliner taken to its peak both in design and performance, and was the biggest

machine of this class produced in the USA for regular airline service.

In comparison to the Super Constellation the Starliner was virtually a new design, although the very low level of engine noise in the cabins, due mainly to powerplant relocation, was reminiscent of the soundproofed Super 'G'. The Super 'G' had been developed with additional insulation and modifications to the propellers which slowed the speed of the tips and this had resulted in a much quieter interior, even in those seats nearest the engine.

Basically the L-1649A was superior to its predecessor chiefly through the use of a new laminar flow wing, improved powerplants,

Below:

Because of the success of the Douglas DC-7C, TWA requested Lockheed to produce an updated Super Constellation to compete. As a result the L-1649P Starliner was built and introduced into TWA service. Pictured here is DC-7C N303AA of American Airlines. *McDonnell Douglas*

Above:
The prototype L-1649 Starliner (c/n 1001) pulls into a tight bank to port on a test flight. The aircraft appropriately carried the civil registration N1649 and made its initial flight on 11 October 1956. *Lockheed*

redesigned functional systems and larger propellers, all features which would produce a new standard of performance, comfort and dependability. Despite all this, however, Lockheed emphasised that with the many changes incorporated into the L-1649A, similarity with previous Constellation models had also been retained as far as possible. For example, there were no major cockpit design or procedural alterations carried out, maintenance and repairs to the powerplants did not differ significantly from the L-1049G Super Constellation, and the basic concepts of systems and components did not depart radically from previous configurations.

The most important element in the advanced performance and capabilities of the Starliner was undoubtedly the newly designed laminar flow wing, which had a span of 150ft — 27ft greater than that of the L-1049G. The aspect ratio was 12:1 as against the 9.17:1 of earlier Constellations, although the dihedral angle of 7° 30' was the same for both the early Super Constellations and the new Starliner. The wing itself was located further aft along the fuselage than that of the L-1049G, and with its large machined parts the L-1649A wing became the nearest to contemporary one-piece construction attained in a component of that size. As a result, scores of detail parts and hundreds of rivets were eliminated, while the ratio of strength to weight was improved.

The new wing was built in two panels, with a joint at the centreline of the aircraft, and because of the beam length it was necessary to splice the front and rear beams at a specific wing station (WS265.680) and the upper and lower skins at WS468.50. The beam webs were spliced at WS505.50 and 595.00 respectively, and it was emphasised that none of the splices were designed as service joints, but in the case of damage to the left or right wing panel it was possible to replace the panel by dismantling the manufacturing joints.

The wing itself provided ample space for integral fuel tanks, the front beam being situated at 15% and the rear beam at 63.5% of the chord. This beam spread, together with the added 27ft span, allowed a greater fuel capacity than the L-1049G, the Starliner containing a maximum of 9,728 US gal which gave a range with maximum payload of 4,940 miles.

Structurally the Starliner's laminar flow wing consisted of upper and lower skins incorporating

spanwise 'planks', these being milled from extrusions or plates and including integral stiffeners. Both the front and rear beam assemblies comprised a lower beam cap with an upright leg, this forming about one-third of the total beam web height, and a machined web plate to which the upper and lower beam caps were attached, the result being a very effective fail-safe design.

The wing box construction employed truss-type ribs composed of extruded truss members and extruded caps, the ribs being attached by 'H' clips to the integral stiffeners of the upper and lower wing panels, the purpose of this being the elimination of fasteners through the integral fuel tank walls. The

tank end ribs were constructed from integrally stiffened extruded webs and extruded upper and lower caps. The rib caps themselves were riveted to machined flats on the inner surface of the skin and no stringer seals were required.

Each of the main undercarriage support ribs was a single forging, and they were situated in the dry bay aft of the inboard engine nacelle and outside the fuel tank area. Access to the dry bay was via a panel in the rear beam directly aft of each dry bay section, while two smaller panels located in the rear beam allowed inspection of the dry bay from outside the area. All external access panels for the fuel tanks were similar to those on the L-1049G, but in the case of the Starliner they were located on top of the wing.

A number of improvements were, however, incorporated into the fuel tank access panels and the adjacent structure to help obviate any possible fuel leakage. The box beam construction made extensive use of faying-surface sealing within the integral tanks without any structural compromise being necessary; all the integral tanks were sealed by the latest contemporary sealants and fill and drain operations. Access to the compass wiring plugs was provided by a panel in the port upper wing surface.

The wing leading-edge on the L-1649A Starliner was divided into sections, two extending from the wing roots to the outboard nacelle. These sections were hinged at the upper beam cap to open upwards and provide easy access to piping, wiring and other equipment mounted on the front wing beam. From the outboard nacelle to the wing tip there were three hinged leading-edge sections,

these having hinges fitted at both the top and bottom. All the leading-edge sections could be removed by pulling out the stainless steel hinge-pins which were quite short and dry-film lubricated. On the two inboard sections each hinge-pin was attached to a small plate, which was in turn fixed to the wing by means of quick-opening fasteners to ensure pin retention. When the hinge-pin was out a red patch was visible, and this was not covered completely until the pin and plate were correctly installed. Each of the leading-edge sections was recessed to allow for the chordwise de-icer boot installations used, and as the sections could easily be removed, de-icer boots could be replaced on the workshop bench.

The trailing-edge skinning consisted of panels which were assembled by means of a metal-bonding process known as Scotchweld, the top skin comprising a smooth outer sheet bonded to a beaded inner sheet, while the bottom skin also consisted of two bonded sheets. A number of closure pans were attached to the underneath of the trailing-edge skin for controlling the air flow between the upper surface of the wing flaps and the trailing-edge itself. This idea narrowed the gap between the trailing-edge and the flaps, thus reducing drag and allowing for improved lift. When the wing flaps were fully extended for servicing

59

Above:
This L-1649A Starliner (c/n 1018) N7316C was also at one time with TWA. It later flew with Alaska Airlines, Flying 'W' Airlines, Prudhoe Bay Oil Distributing Co (Anchorage, Alaska), West Air Inc (Bethel, Alaska) and Burns Aviation Inc. *MAP*

purposes, all equipment fitted to the rear beam face was accessible for maintenance and inspection. In addition 11 hinged and Cam-Loc fastened access panels were located along the lower trailing-edges of each wing, and with ribs in the trailing-edge being spaced from 18-24in apart, plenty of room was available for maintenance purposes. The wingtip was produced as a single unit measuring 28in in length and was fastened to the main wing outer section by four tension bolts. Access to these bolts, as well as to the navigation light plugs and compass transmitters, was by means of a hinged panel in the upper skinning.

The engine nacelles were a semi-monocoque construction built integral with the wing structure, except that they were structurally independent of the wing leading-edge. The nacelles were fitted to the wing front beam by means of a shear and tension structural joint and their main internal framework was formed from 17-7PH steel, while the flat-wrapped skinning was fabricated from 302

full hard stainless steel. Spot-welded construction was used throughout for each nacelle, and the main undercarriage doors on the inboard nacelles were formed from stainless steel skin fitted over an aluminium sub-structure. Engine oil was added from the top of both inner and outer nacelles, while the outboard nacelle contained an alcohol service filler at the top while access to the air conditioning equipment lay below and to the rear.

Fire protection was obviously high on the list of priorities when constructing an aeroplane, especially those built for the carrying of passengers, and with the L-1649A Starliner, Lockheed certainly went to great lengths to prevent any possible fire spreading from one area to another around the nacelles. Compartmentation and barriers were incorporated so that with the inboard nacelles a fireshield of stainless steel was installed some 15in forward of the front wing beam. This covered the front beam installations, yet the fireshield was quite easily removed for maintenance and inspection purposes. The outboard nacelles had fireshielding composed of several small stainless steel sections spaced around 1in from the front wing beam. Equipment fitted on the front beam was in the fire zone in that area and as an added precaution it was constructed from fire-resistant material. Another safety move was the provision of closed trailing-edge ribs on either side of each nacelle and outboard of the cabin heater, while closure was provided between the wing and fuselage in the aft service area compartment. Other measures taken to prevent any possible fire from spreading included

closed leading-edge ribs being installed just outboard of the wing and fuselage fillet, closed fillet bulkheads provided over the box beam near the front and rear wing beams, and closed leading-edge ribs fitted on either side in the stub leading-edge portion of each nacelle.

The main attachment points for joining the wing itself to the fuselage were located on the bottom ends of the circular fuselage bulkhead frames, these being fitted fore and aft on to the front and rear wing beams respectively. Machined pads in each of the bulkhead frame ends married up to forgings bolted to the exposed face of the beams. Double attaching bolts were used (two double bolts for each of the four attachments) to afford the maximum in fail-safe design.

This arrangement, a bolt within a bolt in fact, meant that in the event of one bolt failing, the second was capable of carrying the design load. These special attaching bolts could be readily inspected either by removal of the wing-to-fuselage fillet sections, or by means of cabin floor inspection covers.

In order that the complete wing assembly could be handled both during manufacture and a possible replacement operation in the field, hoist fittings were incorporated in the structure. In addition the whole 150ft span unit, complete with nacelles, could be moved on a special trailer fitted with wing support mountings, the motive power being provided by a towing tractor.

The fuel system comprised seven integral tanks — an outer, centre and inner tank to each wing —

the seventh tank being located in the aircraft's centre-section where it was divided by the port and starboard wing joint. The fuel was thus distributed across the entire wing span, with the exception of the dry bay areas aft of each inboard engine, each wing tank containing some 1,350 and the centre-section tank 1,600 US gal of 115/145 grade gasoline. A vented, vapour-tight, neoprene blanket (septum) separated the upper surfaces of the wing from the fuselage to prevent fumes from entering the cabin area should a leak occur in the centre-section fuel tank.

Electrically-operated fuel booster pumps were mounted in the lower wing portion at the aft end inboard of each tank, these pumps delivering fuel to the engine-driven pumps at pressures of between 19 and 35lb/sq in. Fuel could be supplied from any tank to any engine or combination of engines by means of a crossfeed system, but the design also prevented an inter-tank transfer of fuel from occurring and placed all fuel and vent plumbing within the confines of the box area of the wing.

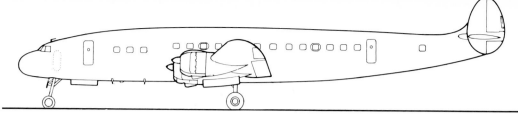

10 Starliner — End of an Era

As has already been stated the L-1649A Starliner, while appearing as virtually a new aeroplane, had a number of features previously used on the L-1049G Super Constellation incorporated in its design. An example was the electrical system, quite similar and comprising a 28V dc single wire arrangement. The airframe structure itself acted as a common ground, although this was not utilised at the flight station circuits, these having two wires to eliminate any possible compass deviation. Additionally the L-1649A employed a secondary 115V three-phase, 400-cycle ac system.

The air conditioning system too was little changed between the Super 'G' and the Starliner; the air distribution, pressurisation, cooling, cabin and cockpit heating and the ventilating methods being similar. However, some of these accessories differed in their location and installation, an example being the main body of the refrigeration system which was situated in the outboard lower nacelles, aft of the wing front beam bulkhead on the L-1649A Starliner. As in the Super 'G' the cabin supercharger was located in the outboard nacelles (zone No 3), and was supported by a welded tube bracket fixed to the wing front beam. Because of the different wing structure on the Starliner, the two cabin heater units — similar to those of the L-1049G — were installed further forward and reversed from their position on the Super 'G'. Another heater unit, which was installed on one side of the L-1049G, was fitted on the opposite side of the Starliner and was reversed end for end.

The L-1649A utilised two 3,000lb/sq in main hydraulic systems which were supplemented by electrically driven auxiliary units. This method achieved the quick action of hydraulic equipment and allowed a reduction in the size and weight of major components, this being particularly noticeable with the undercarriage actuating cylinders. The number one hydraulic system was operated by variable-displacement pumps driven by engines one and three, while system number two was similarly powered from number two and four engines.

Because of the new laminar flow wing it was not possible to install the earlier type of aileron control boosters in the L-1649A Starliner. At the same time, Lockheed was desirous of providing a revised booster unit which would feature improved performance and maintenance characteristics, and so was produced the L-1649A control booster system. This was in fact a modified form of the booster system designed and installed in the Lockheed C-130 Hercules military transport, and it could be installed as a basic unit at the aileron, elevator or rudder positions. The hydraulic components of this new L-1649A booster were grouped in a manifold that could easily be removed from the booster unit, either for a bench check or possible replacement. Lockheed gave an assurance of exceptional reliability from all three boosters, for each had a dual tandem actuating cylinder operated from both hydraulic systems. A single booster unit was employed for both ailerons on the Starliner and was located in the after unpressurised section of the lower fuselage. This one booster operated the ailerons by means of push-pull tubes which were supported by rollers.

Another feature of the Starliner's hydraulic system was the installation of a PB-20A autopilot which had electro-hydraulic controls linked to the booster hydraulic manifold.

The wing flaps also relied on the hydraulic system of the L-1649A for their operation. These flaps had been redesigned to employ two flap sections on each wing, the individual sections being actuated by two ball bearing screw jacks and intermediate gearbox assemblies mounted in the trailing-edges of the wings. Newly designed carriages and tracks were also incorporated for the movement of the Lockheed-Fowler flaps which were operated by two hydraulic motors through a main gearbox. Each of these motors was driven separately by one of the two 3,000lb/sq in main hydraulic systems, a torque tube arrangement linking the drive motors and intermediate gearbox units. Flap positions were selected from the flight deck by a cable system, which in turn connected to a follow-up device mounted on the main gearbox.

With the gross take-off weight of the Starliner having risen to 156,000lb, it was necessary to design a completely new main undercarriage, the locking mechanisms also being redesigned for these new units. The uplocks on all three landing gears could be opened by manual release should there be a failure of the hydraulic system, and the main gear legs were designed for use as a speed brake when released by the manual release cable system at speeds up to 269mph. The nosewheel under-carriage remained essentially the same on the L-1649A as that on the Super 'G' Constellation, the only modification being the provision of two actuating cylinders, each of which was operated separately by one of the two main hydraulic systems.

The increase in wing span of the L-1649A made it possible to move the engine nacelles farther out by a distance of 5ft, this having the consequent effect of reducing interior cabin noise. Noise reduction was also improved by the installation of extra soundproofing material as well as the synchrophas-ing of the Hamilton Standard propellers which, with a slower rate of turns per minute, had a reduced blade tip speed, thus greatly lowering audible airscrew throb.

Power for the Starliner was provided by four 3,400hp Wright 988TC-18EA-2 Turbo-Compound radials, just about the most powerful piston engines ever used in a production civil aircraft in service. These powerplants each drove a three-blade Hamilton Standard metal propeller of 16ft 10in diameter, but having a tip-to-fuselage clearance in excess of 5ft.

The whole of the tail unit on the Starliner was alike in profile and dimensions to earlier Constel-lations, with the exception of the tailplane chord which was slightly increased. However, some structural changes became necessary in order that new reinforcing members could be incorporated to support the rudder and elevator hydraulic booster units introduced on this model. The counter-balances were also removed from the control horns and installed at the tops of the rudders below the uppermost hinges. Other empennage modifications included strengthening of the stabiliser beams and minor changes to the leading-edge structure and rudder torque tubes.

With its weather radar nose the fuselage of the Starliner was 2ft 7in longer than the earlier L-1049C

Below:
In this dramatic night scene at Orly Airport, Paris, L-1649A Starliner of Air France (c/n 1020) F-BHBL, prepares for a transatlantic flight to the United States. *Air France*

Super Constellation, the radar being housed within the non-metal cone which was normally in matt black finish and attached to the extreme front pressure bulkhead of the L-1649A.

Considerable structural redesigning was necessary with the Starliner, chiefly because of the need to accommodate the new laminar flow wing and adjust to the increase in maximum weight of the aircraft. Much of this work involved part of the fuselage known as number 4 section — originally barrel-shaped — which was altered to have a cross-section constant in diameter, while section 5A, aft of section 4, had to be re-faired so that it would match up to the revised cylindrical shape of the modified portion.

Service areas in the lower fuselage, forward and aft of the wing junctions, were not pressurised and access to these places was by means of hinged doors fitted into the bottom centre-line of the aircraft. The forward servicing area contained a majority of the hydraulic system units and a reserve oil tank, while in the rear servicing area could be found the aileron booster unit, wing flap and aileron actuating devices and the ground/air conditioning connection.

Accommodation aboard the Starliner was after the style of the Super 'G' Constellation, the flight deck housing the captain, first officer, radio operator and flight engineer. Aft of them the navigator sat on the port side of a small compartment in which the opposite side was given up to a crew rest area. Entrance for the crew was via a starboard door which provided direct access to the flight deck.

The forward passenger cabin was situated immediately aft of the navigator's position and crew rest area, a central door in the cabin bulkhead giving access from the flight deck area to the front passenger compartment. At the rear of the forward cabin were located port and starboard toilets with wardrobes, a centre aisle leading between them to the main passenger cabin, where a sloping floor led over the centre-section to the after end of this compartment. Admittance to a lounge area was then provided by another centre doorway through a bulkhead, while the next bulkhead to the rear allowed access to the same lounge from the passenger entrance lobby. The main entry door to the lobby was locked by multiple bolts linked to a single handle once the aircraft was ready for take-off. Behind the entrance lobby rear bulkhead was the rearmost passenger cabin followed by wardrobes, washrooms and finally the port and starboard toilets, which were located immediately in front of the fuselage production break-line.

A galley was situated on the starboard side of the aircraft opposite the main passenger entry door, and from it the cabin staff could serve hot and cold meals, while coffee that had been preheated before a flight was kept in insulated containers in the galley from where it was dispensed piping hot. The cabin staff themselves were provided with folding seats for their own convenience, these being located in a small area aft of the rearmost passenger cabin.

The Starliner contained a useful 593cu ft of cargo space divided between a forward and rear freight/baggage hold incorporated into the lower fuselage beneath the front and rear passenger

Left and below:
Contemporaries of the Super Constellation and Starliner under construction at Lockheed included the P2V Neptune, this example being a P2V-4 with six 20mm cannon in the nose; and the Lockheed F-94C Starfire, its single Pratt & Whitney J48-P-5 jet engine developing 8,300lb of thrust. *MAP*

compartments. Fitted in the under-belly area ahead of the centre-section was a marker beacon, twin ADF loops, radar safety beacon (IFF), radio and altimeter antenna and the ADF sense aerial. A VOR antenna and HF radio aerial were fitted in the flight deck roof, the HF mast being equipped with a de-icing boot, while a VHF antenna was placed in a dorsal position.

Like the Super 'G' Constellation, the Starliner was equipped with pneumatically-operated de-icer boots fitted integrally on all leading-edges including the triple fins. For service and maintenance purposes the leading- and trailing-edges of the wings, as well as the tips, were no-step areas, servicing points being accessible from the centre portions of the wing. There were four fuel-filling positions on top of the starboard wing and three on the port wing, while engine oil was replenished via fillers in the top of each powerplant, a 45 US gal capacity oil tank being installed in each engine for which the recommended grade of oil was 120

(Wright Aero Div Spec 5815). On top of the outboard engines were located the fillers for the alcohol used in the anti-icing system, these service fillers being aft of the oil filler location to the rear of the nacelle where there was an anti-icing service area. Each of the two alcohol tanks had a 20 US gal capacity.

By the time construction was started on the Starliner, factory space at Lockheed's Burbank plant alone had increased over the years to no less than 2 million sq ft. Much of this was given over to Super Constellation and subsequently Starliner production, but this availability also included indirect facilities as administrative, tooling, engineering and general services which were also applied to other contemporary types being produced including the P2V Neptune anti-submarine patrol bomber, the T-33 jet trainer, F-94C Starfire fighter and the C-130 Hercules transport. Space directly involved with Super Constellation production, including the military R7V-1s, WV-2s and

RC-121Cs, totalled 700,000sq ft for actual assembly lines, plus another 250,000sq ft for the fabrication of components exclusively for the Super Constellations, these facilities being envisaged as readily available for L-1649A Starliner production. In addition to the Burbank plant, however, Lockheed's California Division also included factories at Bakersfield, Palmdale, Beverly Hills and Van Nuys, total floor space in the division equalling 5,976,000sq ft. Another plant operated at Marietta, Georgia, where some 4,455,000sq ft of floor space was available, and in that facility Lockheed produced their own C-130 Hercules turbo-prop transport and Boeing B-47 Stratojet bombers under contract.

The company also ran two training schools especially intended for the use of civil and military operators of the Constellation family and ensuing Starliner. One school was devoted to Flight Operations, the other functioning as a Service Group. The Flight Operations unit concentrated on instruction in specific features of the aircraft which would be of interest especially to pilots and flight engineers, the idea being that optimum performance could be gained from the day the machine was delivered. The Service Group unit specialised in familiarising customers' personnel with maintenance procedures and techniques on Lockheed's latest airliner models. One example was a course entitled 'Line Maintenance', this being any crew chief's curriculum to cover the entire aircraft. Both groups used actual Super Constellations or L-1649As in various stages of construction for familiarisation, while numbers of components were made up as operating models including panels, gauges, levers and controls.

Additionally Lockheed specialists were stationed strategically in those parts of the world where the airliners operated in order that they would be on hand to assist the airline operators themselves. Thus through periodic and special visits these field representatives were able to liaise between Lockheed and the operator on maintenance and engineering information. Where a customer was introducing the Super Constellation or Starliner into service, a Lockheed company specialist was assigned to that airline for a definite period.

On 11 October 1956 the prototype Starliner took off from Burbank on its maiden flight. Suitably allotted the civil registration N1649 it carried a crew headed by R. Wimmer and H. R. Salmon, no problems being encountered. A series of test flights were then undertaken during which N1649 made over 100 trips across the blue waters of the Pacific Ocean. This test flight programme proved beyond doubt the advantages of the new laminar flow wing as well as those of the improved powerplants, redesigned functional systems and the larger, slower-turning, three-blade propellers. The L-1649 had obviously reached a pinnacle in the development of piston-engined passenger-carrying aircraft and it was responsible for the introduction of new standards in comfort, performance and dependability in aeroplanes of that category. It accommodated 58 first class (later 62), or 75 tourist class (later 92 and eventually 99) passengers.

As with earlier Constellation variants, TWA was first in the queue to purchase the production version of the Starliner, the L-1649A, and designated it their 'Jetstream' class. The first TWA Starliner to enter service (c/n 1002) had originally been used in the type's certification programme which had been successfully concluded and approved on 27 March 1957, and after delivery to TWA it was named *Star of Wyoming*, the civil registration being N7301C and the TWA fleet No 301.

With its superb range the Starliner was an obvious choice for the North Atlantic route, and on 1 June 1957 TWA commenced their New York-London-Paris service, Frankfurt being added just one month later. On 30 September the same year a new service was inaugurated from San Francisco on America's west coast to London, a distance of 5,500 miles, this flight taking just over 18½hr. Other record flights were accomplished with the Starliner, thanks to its new wing, and these included a Burbank to Paris trip made in 16hr 21min, while among similar flights from Burbank to Europe were those to Hamburg and London. Another Starliner flight was from New York to Athens, and in addition to TWA the L-1649A was used by Air France, Lufthansa, Trek Airways, Condor Flugdienst and World Airways.

Potential for a long production run of the Starliner looked promising, but the type was too late an arrival on the world airline scene. The jet-engined Boeings and DC-8s were entering service in ever-increasing numbers and the days of the big piston-engined airliners were over as far as the major operators were concerned. It was the end of an era which has been on a par with the earlier golden age of the flying-boats.

Top left:
Here is another fine view of the prototype L-1649 Starliner near the Californian coast while on test. Note the pronounced dihedral on the laminar flow wings with their 150ft span. *Lockheed*

Left:
Naming it their Jetstream class, TWA were first to purchase the L-1649A Starliner, putting the type into service on the New York-London-Paris route on 1 June 1957. This is another fine shot of TWA's N7301C, which was to be named *Star of Wyoming*. *Lockheed*

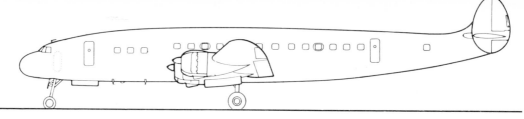

11 Major Airlines and the Constellation

Prior to World War 2, Transcontinental and Western Air (TWA) had operated only on domestic routes in the United States. However, after 5 July 1945 the company's horizons were broadened considerably with the granting by the Civil Aeronautics Bureau of two international routes. The new services would be able to fly from the major US cities of Boston, Chicago, Detroit, New York, Philadelphia and Washington to Europe and beyond. The first stop would be at Gander, Newfoundland, to refuel, and from there a scheduled northern or southern route was to operate across the Atlantic to Cairo and eventually India. The northern route flew to Ireland (refuel), Paris, Geneva, Rome and Athens before reaching Cairo, while the southern service was via Lisbon, Algiers, Tunis, Tripoli and Benghazi. A link was provided between the two routes which operated from Lisbon to Rome via Madrid. When the TWA route to Bombay from Cairo commenced it flew via Tel Aviv, Basra and Dhahran.

The first scheduled international service operated by TWA was inaugurated on 5 February 1946 when a Lockheed L-049 Constellation, N86511 *Star of Paris* (c/n 2035), took off from New York's La Guardia Airport en route for Paris. It carried 36 passengers, a crew of eight and some cargo; with refuelling stops at Gander and Shannon (Eire) the flight took 19hr 46min, the pilot on that occasion being TWA's Capt Harold F. Blackburn. This aircraft was one of 27 L-049s ordered by TWA shortly after the end of the war with Japan, and because it had been responsible for much of the Constellation's development, the airline was given priority in order of delivery and more or less guaranteed the first 12 L-049s to be produced by Lockheed. Indeed the first was delivered on 15 November and by the end of the year TWA had taken delivery of a further nine machines.

On the day prior to TWA's inaugural New York to Paris service, the airlines president Jack Frye had flown a Constellation from Burbank, California, to

New York (La Guardia) in a record time of 7hr 28min. Just 10 days later on 15 February 1946, Howard Hughes himself piloted the *Star of California*, another L-049, from Los Angeles to New York in 8hr 38min. This flight inaugurated TWA's American coast-to-coast service with Constellations. On the same day TWA commenced its scheduled service to Rome via Gander, Shannon and Paris, the Constellation doing the honours on this occasion being NC86510, named appropriately *Star of Rome* (c/n 2034).

For its inaugural service to Cairo on 1 April 1946, TWA used a Douglas DC-4 aircraft named *The Acropolis* flying from Washington DC to Egypt via New York, Gander, Shannon, Paris, Rome and Athens. In just under 29hr the DC-4 had landed at Payne Field, Cairo (now Cairo International Airport), but the following month on 3 May, TWA introduced the L-049 Constellation as the only type on its Egyptian route, starting from Chicago and flying to Cairo via New York, Gander, Shannon and European cities.

The last L-049 Constellation delivered to TWA was N90826 (c/n 2088), fleet No 515, and carried the name *Star of the China Sea*, this machine coming off Lockheed's assembly line during 1946. Because of an airline pilots' strike in October 1947, TWA cancelled eight L-049s ordered and, even worse for Lockheed, a contract worth $20 million for 18 of the model L-649 Constellation.

A year later TWA introduced an all-sleeper Constellation service on its New York to Paris route, and in 1950 (the same year as the company phased out its DC-4s on international routes) the old name of Transcontinental and Western Air was changed to Trans World Airlines, thus retaining the old initials TWA.

In the Constellation TWA had a pressurised aircraft capable of carrying up to 47 passengers on its transatlantic service at a cruising speed of 270mph. This was faster, higher and more

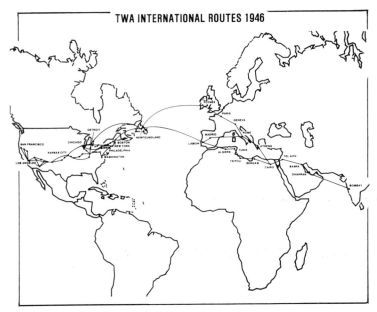

TWA INTERNATIONAL ROUTES 1946

Left:
**This official TWA map shows
the extent of the company's
expansion during 1946. The
link between the northern and
southern routes can be seen
stretching from Lisbon to
Rome via Madrid.** *TWA*

Below:
**This significant picture was
taken on 5 February 1946 and
shows TWA L-049
Constellation *Star of Paris*
(c/n 2035) NC86511, fleet
No 555, about to depart from
La Guardia Airport, New York.
This was the inaugural flight of
TWA's New York to Paris
service via Gander and
Shannon, the aircraft carrying
36 passengers, eight crew
members and some
cargo.** *TWA*

comfortable than the earlier DC-4 service, and in 1952 TWA's Constellations were modified to accommodate up to 60 passengers, thus enabling the company to inaugurate its transatlantic 'Sky Tourist' service for 'coach' class passengers.

Meanwhile Pan American Airways (renamed Pan American World Airways in 1950) had ordered 22 Lockheed Model L-049 Constellations on 23 October 1945, the first machine — N88831 (c/n 2031) — being delivered to the airline on 5 January 1946. Just under one month later on 3 February, Pan Am introduced the Constellation into service on their New York to Bermuda route.

By the end of 1949, L-049 Connies had replaced the Boeing Model 314A Yankee Clipper flying-boats on Pan Am's service between San Francisco and Honolulu, and were soon operating the company's other service to Natal, Brazil, Lisbon, Dakar, Monrovia and Leopoldville (Belgian Congo). Pan Am also flew the North Atlantic route starting in February 1946, linking New York (La Guardia) with London (then served by Hurn Airport) via Gander and Shannon with L-049 Constellations.

A subsidiary of Pan Am was Panair do Brasil, and three L-049 Connies were supplied to that airline by

the parent company, the first aircraft (c/n 2049) being delivered direct to Rio de Janeiro on 31 March 1946. This machine, initially allotted the registration N88849, was given the Brazilian registration PP-PCF and named *Manoel de Borba Gato*. It carried out a proving flight from Rio to London via Recife and Dakar on 16 April, and on landing at London's new Heathrow Airport became the first aircraft belonging to a foreign airline to do so.

Panair do Brasil's first scheduled Constellation service to London from Rio de Janeiro commenced on 27 April 1946, and in the same year as more new Constellations were delivered, the Rio to Europe routes were extended to Paris (1 July) and Rome (3 October). In 1947, the airline's services operated to Cairo (5 June) and Istanbul (16 November), while on 9 March the following year the Paris route was extended to Frankfurt, West Germany.

The Model L-049 and L-149 Constellation became Panair do Brasil's flagships from early 1946 until the mid-1950s, and by the end of April 1949 the type had completed more than 1,000 crossings of the South Atlantic. On 5 October the Istanbul route was extended to Beirut, and in 1951 the South American network which already included

Montevideo and Buenos Aires took in Santiago, Chile and Lima, the capital of Peru. Panair do Brasil was able to claim a record on 30 December 1953 when one of its Constellations made a scheduled nonstop flight from Lisbon to Rio de Janeiro, a distance of 4,837 miles, in 21hr 40min. Previously that year, on 31 August, the airline had added Hamburg to its list of European destinations, and on 22 March 1954 a service to Dusseldorf was included.

Meanwhile during 1946 in Great Britain, British Overseas Airways Corporation (BOAC) was facing a dilemma. Requiring a new and suitable aircraft of British origin for its North Atlantic route, the Corporation was hoping to acquire a fleet of Avro Tudor Is, a pressurised design powered by four Rolls-Royce Merlin 621 engines. However, the Tudor I, which was built to carry only 12 passengers across the North Atlantic, had suffered a lengthy gestation period and still retained a number of aerodynamic problems. At a meeting on 12 March 1946 BOAC stipulated over 340 modifications they would require to the Tudor, and just over a year later on 11 April 1947 they cancelled the Tudor contract.

With no other British airliner design immediately available at that time (the Handley Page Hermes

was nearly four years away) BOAC placed an order for eight Lockheed L-049 Constellations, the first of which — G-AHEJ (c/n 1975) and named *Bristol II* — was introduced on BOAC's New York to London service via Gander and Shannon. When first put into service the BOAC Constellations had basically an overall natural metal finish, but this was replaced by the well-known white fuselage top carrying the letters BOAC each side, and the black cheat line. The speedbird emblem was carried on the outer rudders with the individual aircraft registration below it. Each BOAC Connie was allotted a name, this being painted in white beneath the cockpit on each side. A typical example was G-AHEM (c/n 1978) which was named *Balmoral*. Later, between 1948 and 1955, BOAC acquired a further 17 Constellations, these being the updated L-749A version.

The Australian airline QANTAS was another firm believer in the capabilities of the Lockheed Constellation. In October 1946 QANTAS placed an order with Lockheed for four new L-749 Constellations at a total cost of $5½ million. The aircraft arrived a year later and were made ready for a weekly service on the original 'Kangaroo' service to London via Singapore, this having reopened 18 months earlier in April 1946. At about that time QANTAS had just become an entirely Australian-owned concern, the old Imperial Airways half-share having been acquired from that airline's successor (BOAC) by the Australian Government. Then on 3 July 1947 the remaining local shareholding was bought up by the government also, and QANTAS became Australia's national overseas air service. Five months later on 1 December 1947, the first QANTAS Constellation VH-EAA (c/n 2562) named *Ross Smith*, took off from Kingsford Smith Airport, Sydney, on the first leg of its flight to London. This flight also introduced the first QANTAS stewardess service for passengers.

It was this same aircraft (VH-EAA) that had caused quite a stir when it arrived on its delivery flight from the United States. This was made in the record time of 43hr (elapsed) and 33hr (flying), and waiting to greet the aircraft and its crew were the Australian Minister for Air Mr Drakeford, Mr Hudson Fysh (chairman and managing director of QANTAS) and Sir Keith Smith who, with his brother Ross, had made the first flight between England and Australia in 1919 flying a Vickers Vimy.

Those watching the graceful new airliner were amazed when it actually reversed into position in front of the Kingsford Smith terminal building — it was the first aircraft in Australia with reversible pitch propellers. Pressurisation was also something new in a passenger aircraft in Australia, as was the 'floating' cabin described by one reporter as a cabin within a cabin with the entire wall of the passenger section floating free of the main aircraft structure on a bed of rubber. Aviation writer Norman Ellison described the Constellation in the Sydney *Sun* and stated: 'The Constellations have more new features than any other airliner in a decade. They add up to greater speed, a higher degree of safety, more comfort, and bigger and better menus'. With the latter of course came the newly introduced stewardesses, or air hostesses as they became known.

In 1952 QANTAS Constellations inaugurated the fortnightly 'Wallaby' service between Sydney and Johannesburg, thus providing for Australia, which had been virtually isolated by World War 2, a second strategic route to the UK. The following year saw the coronation of Her Majesty Queen Elizabeth II, and to honour the great occasion all QANTAS Constellations on the Sydney to London service proudly carried the Coronation crest and conveyed special Coronation airmail souvenirs.

Below:
A TWA hostess prepares to serve dinner from the galley aboard a TWA L-049 Constellation in 1946. Coffee was prepared in flight kitchens on the ground and kept hot on board the aircraft in insulated containers as seen here. *TWA*

Further honours were to befall QANTAS in 1954 when Her Majesty the Queen visited Australia. Together with the Duke of Edinburgh, Her Majesty was flown on her Australian tour in L-749 Constellation VH-EAF (c/n 2504) named *Horace Brinsmead*, after the first Controller of Civil Aviation in Australia. During the Royal tour, Hudson Fysh, an original pioneer of QANTAS, was made a Knight of the British Empire, the ceremony taking place at Government House, Sydney. This was the first investiture ever held by a British Sovereign in Australia.

Air France was one of the first European airlines to put its faith in the Constellation, an initial order for four L-049s being placed in October 1945. These replaced Air France's Douglas DC-4s on the Paris to New York service, the first Constellation flight leaving Paris on 3 January 1947. There then followed a period of rapid expansion for the company with further supplies of Constellations arriving as they became available. These included the Model L-749 and L-749A and routes were flown to South America, the Far East, Australasia, Mexico City and the French West Indies. By the start of 1953 these routes were established and from the French West Indies further services could be extended to Colombia and Venezuela. Scheduled flights to Montreal, Canada, had been inaugurated on 20 October 1950, while the service to Mexico began on 27 April 1952. By 1954 Air France was operating 21 L-749 Constellations, although more modern types were beginning to enter service; even in the summer of 1959 there were still 15 L-749s operating at a time when the number of passengers carried had increased over a 10-year period by an annual average rate of 14%, much of that growth being due to the introduction into Air France service of the Lockheed Constellation from early 1947 onwards.

A number of other well known international airlines decided to adopt the Lockheed Constellation for their postwar services, among which was Air India. This company received its first L-749 Connie on 30 January 1948, the aircraft (c/n 2504) being registered VT-CQS and named *Mogul Princess*. On 8 June Air India commenced its Constellation service from Bombay to London via Cairo and Geneva, and by the time the airline was nationalised on 1 August 1953 London was being served by four flights a week — two from Bombay and two from Calcutta. In the ensuing years Air India's routes would extend to the USA, East Africa, Far East, Australia and the Soviet Union.

In the United States, Eastern Air Lines (EAL) had ordered their first Lockheed L-049 Constellation on 10 September 1945, but this contract was altered later to provide the Model L-649, although a dozen ex-TWA and one ex-Pan Am L-049s flew with EAL. The first of the L-649s arrived with the company on

Above:
L-049 Constellation F-BAZD (c/n 2075) taxies past the camera in 1947 prior to delivery to Air France. Notice the c/n on the nose of the aircraft and the open engine cooling gills. *Air France*

Left:
A superb close-up of the Wright GR-3350-749C18BD-1 Cyclone radials and Curtiss electric propellers on an Air India L-749 at Heathrow in the early 1950s. *Air India*

19 March 1947, to be followed by a further 13 machines so that by May EAL's L-649s were in regular service on the company's routes. Another American operator, Delta Air Lines, merged with Chicago and Southern Air Lines on 1 May 1953 and in so doing acquired a much larger network including international routes. Delta also took over a number of new aircraft which had been ordered by Chicago and Southern, but which awaited delivery, among them six Lockheed L-649A Constellations to be used on the international services. Later, in the early part of 1956, Delta Air Lines began operating to New York and Washington from its Atlanta, Georgia, base, and for this purpose four L-049 Constellations were acquired from Pan Am.

In Great Britain, a company known as Euravia was formed in December 1961, and 5 May the following year commenced a charter service with an L-049 Constellation (c/n 1967) registered G-ARVP. This aircraft flew initially on a Manchester to Palma via Perpignan charter, and by the end of the year had been joined by another seven Constellations including four L-049s and three L-749As. Two of the L-749As were acquired from Skyways of London Ltd, these being G-ALAK (c/n 2548) and G-ALAL (c/n 2549). During 1964 Euravia became Britannia Airways.

KLM Royal Dutch Airlines purchased six L-049, 13 L-749 and seven L-749A Constellations. The L-049s replaced KLM's DC-4s on the Amsterdam to New York service during November 1946, while other new routes were undertaken to Curaçao (Netherlands Antilles) in the Caribbean and Brazil. By 1953 Constellations had been responsible for a large expansion of the KLM network.

In the Middle East Israel's national airline El Al, which had formed on 11 November 1948, purchased three Lockheed L-049 Constellations in June 1950, these being registered 4X-AKA/AKB/AKC (c/n 1965, 1967 and 1968 respectively). They arrived in Tel Aviv during May 1951 and on 16th of that month began an Israel to New York service via Athens or Rome, and London. On 1 October 1953, El Al commenced a service to South Africa by which time another three L-049s had been added to the fleet, these being 4X-AKD/AKE/AKF (c/n 1980, 2061 and 2036 respectively).

Royal Air Maroc (RAM) did not receive its first Constellation, an L-749A (c/n 2512) registered CN-CCR, until October 1957, with three more of the same model being delivered in 1960 and a fifth machine during 1962. Constellations were being acquired to replace RAM's DC-4s on its international routes.

Above left:
One of Eastern Airlines' ('The Great Silver Fleet') L-649 Connies (c/n 2519) NC102A makes haste over the Rickenbacker Causeway. Eastern were first to order the L-649, but the aircraft in this picture was to be modernised to L-749A standard later. *Eastern Air Lines*

Left:
Lockheed L-749A (c/n 2641) PH-LDE (formerly PH-TFE) of KLM taxiing past the camera in 1959. Constellations were responsible for much of KLM's international expansion after World War 2. *MAP*

12 The Connie in Latin America and on Secondary Routes

Since the introduction of the aeroplane in the vast continent of South America, an air link has provided the most practical form of transportation between one area of population and another. Separated by immense stretches of jungle, mountain ranges and plains, many towns and villages could only be reached by an aircraft. In the early days when one, or perhaps two, engines were the thing, this could be a pretty hazardous undertaking by even the best pilot over such hostile terrain. However, after World War 2 the arrival on the scene of the four-engined piston transport aircraft helped to transform the South American way of life. Far more people and greater quantities of cargo could be flown between the communities spread out as they were, and perhaps more important the way was clear for a fast and efficient means of international travel for South Americans, while a great increase in the amount of export freight which could be conveyed very quickly was made possible.

The main bulk of the new transports consisted of Douglas DC-4 Skymasters and Lockheed Constellations, many of which were destined to serve for two decades or more in Latin American countries

— the term Latin America here to include Mexico, Central America and the Caribbean area.

A Mexico City to New York service by Constellation was started on 16 December 1957 by Aeronaves de Mexico, which had formed in 1952 after the merger of a number of small airlines, and which was to become one of Mexico's two national air services. Initially they leased two L-049 Constellations from Pan Am, these being registered as XA-MAG (c/n 2052) and XA-MAH (c/n 2059) for use on the New York route. During 1958, a further four Constellations were acquired by Aeronaves de Mexico, these being Model L-749As registered as XA-MEW (c/n 2619), XA-MEU (c/n 2620), XA-MEV (c/n 2665) and XA-MOA (c/n NA); the first machine (XA-MEW) was named *Acapulco*.

Meanwhile further south in Colombia, that country's well established airline AVIANCA had commenced its initial international service on 21 March 1946 with DC-3 flights to Ecuador, and on 22 January the following year the airline's first long distance, nonstop service was inaugurated to Miami by DC-4s. Two years later this route was extended to New York, and by 1950 AVIANCA has spread its network to include transatlantic services

Left:
Originally with BOAC as G-ANUY, this Lockheed L-749A Constellation (c/n 2557) later went to the Colombian airline AVIANCA as HK-651. Eventually it ended up with Trans Peruana as OB-R-915 and was withdrawn from service in 1969. *MAP*

to Lisbon, Rome and Paris. After 1950 Lockheed Constellations began to join AVIANCA's fleet, six Model L-749As making it possible to add Madrid, Hamburg and Frankfurt to the company's European destinations, while Caracas (Venezuela) and San Juan (Puerto Rico) became intermediate stops in April 1954 and June 1957 respectively. On 1 June 1957 a new service was opened to the Peruvian capital of Lima, this route including a stop at Quito (Ecuador). AVIANCA's L-749As were registered HK-162 (c/n 2663), HK-163 (c/n 2664), HK-650 (c/n 2544), HK-651 (c/n 2557), HK-652 (c/n 2564) and HK-653 (c/n 2645).

Over in Cuba, once it had gained its independence from Pan Am, the island's airline Cubana began expanding its services to include Spain, a route to Madrid from Havana via the Azores commencing in April 1948 with DC-4 aircraft. As traffic increased and further routes were added, Cubana introduced three Lockheed L-049 Connies to its fleet, these being primarily intended to operate a service between Havana and Mexico City via Merida (Venezuela). Two of the Cuban Constellations were registered CU-T-547 (c/n 2036) — an ex-Pan Am aircraft — and CU-T-532 (c/n 2061).

Another airline which began replacing its DC-4s with Lockheed Constellations was the Mexican company Aerovias Guest. Having flown a trans-atlantic service to Spain (Madrid) with its DC-4s from 1948, Aerovias Guest was to cease its Spanish venture in 1951, the route taken having included (from Mexico City) Miami, Bermuda, the Azores and Lisbon. Instead the airline made a concentrated effort to gain traffic on its Miami service, the so-called 'Route of the Sun' between Mexico City and the Florida resort. This endeavour proved very successful, so much so that Aerovias Guest acquired four Model L-749 Constellations to replace the unpressurised and slower DC-4s with the first Connie entering the service during the second week of November 1955. A direct service to Panama was already operating and this route was extended to Caracas (Venezuela) during April 1958. The four L-749 Constellations involved were XA-GOQ (c/n 2053), XA-GOS (c/n na), XA-LIO (c/n 2572) and XA-LIP (c/n 2573), the latter two aircraft being Model L-749As, while the first machine (XA-GOQ) was named *Veracruz*.

One of Venezuela's important airlines has, since its formation in January 1935, been Linea Aeropostal Venezolana (LAV), and with expansion in the years following World War 2 the company was able to purchase a number of new aircraft types including Lockheed Model L-049s and L-749s. The Constellations were used to inaugurate LAV's new international routes from Caracas (Maiquetia) to New York and Port of Spain (Trinidad), and later in November 1953 the Constellations began operating LAV's new transatlantic services to Rome,

Lisbon and Madrid. A service to Panama was also started, but like the Mexican Aerovias Guest concern, LAV found the Miami route far more lucrative than the New York run and the latter service was dropped. One of LAV's L-049s, registered as N90926 (c/n 2064), was initially with American Overseas Airlines (AOA) and named *Chicago*, but AOA leased it to LAV from whom it later passed to Pan Am as *Clipper Ocean Herald*. The other Constellations in the LAV fleet included two L-049s registered YV-C-AME (c/n 2081) named *Simon Bolivar* and YV-C-AMI (c/n 2082) named *Francisca de Miranda*. These aircraft carried the fleet Nos 302 and 301 respectively. Two L-749s were also added in 1947, these machines being registered as YV-C-AMA (c/n 2560) named *Jose Marti* and YV-C-AMU (c/n 2561) named *Antonio Jose de Sucre*.

For a number of years the northern Caribbean area was the haunt of half a dozen Constellations belonging to Aerovias Quisqueyana of the Dominican Republic, this airline lasting from its formation in 1962 until the cessation of operations in 1980. The fleet consisted of three L-049s and three L-749As as follows: L-049 (c/n 2070) HI-260, originally PH-TAW of KLM and then N6000C *Star of Newfoundland* of TWA; L-049 (c/n 2075) N9414H, originally F-BAZD of Air France before passing to TWA as *Star of Lebanon*; L-049 (c/n 2085) NI-270, previously with TWA as N90823 *Star of the Yellow Sea*; L-749A (c/n 2520) HI-140, originally built as L-649 for EAL (N103A, fleet No 103) and retrofitted to L-749 standards; L-749A (c/n 2522) HI-207, originally built as L-649 for EAL (N105A, fleet No 105) and retrofitted to L-749 standards; L-749A (c/n 2523) HI-129, originally built as L-649 for EAL (N106A, fleet No 106) and retrofitted to L-749 standards.

Another company from the Dominican Republic to operate its Constellations in the Caribbean was ARGO SA, which was still using one of its Connies on charter flights to the Antilles and to Miami in the early 1980s. Two of the L-749As operated by the company are known to have been HI-328 (c/n 2607) and HI-393 (c/n 2603), both ex-USAF

C-121As serial Nos 48-615 and 48-611 respectively.

An airline founded in Peru during 1964, but which lasted only for nine years was COPISA (Compania Peruana Internacional de Aviacion SA). This company used Lockheed L-749As on its routes which included Lima, Cali (Colombia), Panama and Miami. In 1967 a service was started to Iquitos on the Amazon and to Maracaibo (Venezuela), but COPISA had to suspend operations for three months that year, services continuing afterwards until the cessation of operations in 1973. Those L-749As known to have been used by COPISA included OB-R-819 (c/n 2523), built originally as an L-649 for EAL, but retrofitted to L-749 standard and also used by Aerovias Quisqueyana; N1949

(c/n 2565), initially with BOAC as G-ANUR, then to Ace Freighters, Skyways of London Ltd, QANTAS as VH-EAB and Aerolineas Uruguayas as CX-BHC in 1968; OB-R-802 (c/n 2566), initially with BOAC as G-ALAO, also Aer Lingus as EI-ADE and Capitol Airways Inc (later Capitol International Airways) with US registration N4902C; OB-R-898 (c/n 2627), originally to Air France as F-BAZN, RAM as CN-CCP; N1939 (c/n 2630), which originally flew with SAA as ZS-DBS. Two other L-749As ordered by COPISA (c/ns 2548 and 2549) were not delivered.

Also in Peru, there was founded in 1963 at Lima a small airline calling itself Lineas Aereas Nacionales SA (LANSA). As well as operating services to other Peruvian areas of population, LANSA began

a series of special tourist flights to such places of interest as the ruins at Chan-Chan and Iquitos on the Amazon. Among its fleet of aircraft LANSA numbered three Lockheed L-749 Constellations, these being all ex-EAL machines as follows: OB-WAA, fleet No 732 (c/n 2614) — ex-EAL N117A; OB-WAB, fleet No 733 (c/n 2518) — ex-EAL N101A; OB-WAC, fleet No 740 (c/n 2534) — ex-EAL N113A. Later these three Connies were re-registered as OB-R-732, OB-R-733 and OB-R-740 respectively in LANSA service.

In addition to the large Panair do Brasil company mentioned in the previous chapter and the more prominent South American airlines referred to here, there were of course numerous other small and less well known operators of first generation Constellations in the Latin American area. A brief summary of some of these concerns would not, therefore, be amiss here and can include the following: Aerolineas Carreras Transportes Aereos of Argentina, which flew L-749A LV-PBH (c/n 2619), later re-registered as LV-IIC; Aerolineas Uruguayas of Uruguay, operated L-749A CX-BHC (c/n 2565), with an option on L-749A CX-BHD (c/n 2548) which was not proceeded with; Aerotransportes Entre Rios SRL of Argentina, with L-749A LV-PZX (c/n 2540), later re-registered as LV-IGS; Air Haiti International flew L-749A HH-ABA (c/n 2615) during 1961 until the aircraft was lost at sea in November of that year; Arruda of Brazil operated L-049 (c/n 2037) with the registration PP-PDG from

Top:

Although in Euravia service in this picture, this L-749A (c/n 2565) G-ANUR was sold later to Aerolineas Uruguayas of Uruguay, and flew with the registration CX-BHC. MAP

Above:

Having ended its career in 1969 this rather cannibalised L-749A has been withdrawn from service by its last owners, Trans Peruana of Peru, with whom it was registered OB-R-802 MAP

1971 until the machine crashed in May the following year; CAUSA of Uruguay which operated three L-749A Connies, CX-BBM (c/n 2661), CX-BBN (c/n 2641) and CX-BCS (c/n 2640), between 1962-67; Lineas Aereas de Panama SA ordered four L-049s — RX-121 (c/n 1968), RX-123 (c/n 1965) which was not delivered, RX-124 (c/n 1967) and one other for spares (c/n 1962); Lloyd Aero Paraguayo SA (LAPSA) flew L-049 Constellation ZP-CAS (c/n 1964) from December 1963 until the following month when it crashed and had to be abandoned; Rutas Internacionales Peruanas SA (RIPSA) of Lima, Peru, which ordered two L-749As but flew only one — OB-R-833 (c/n 2610), the option on the second machine (c/n 2522) not being taken up; Rymar of Montevideo, Uruguay, flew L-049 in 1965, this aircraft being registered as N86533 (c/n 2071); Trans-Peruana de Aviacion SA of Lima, Peru, which between 1967 and 1970 flew four L-749As — OB-R-914 (c/n 2544), OB-R-915 (c/n 2557), OB-R-916 (c/n 2564) and OB-R-917 (c/n 2645).

In the Dominican Republic a company known as Transporte Aereo Dominicano SA (TRADO) operated two Constellations during 1979 and 1980. The first was a Model L-049 (c/n 2070) registered HI-260, and the second an L-749A (c/n 2522) registered HI-332. A third aircraft was purchased, another L-049 (c/n 2085) allotted the registration HI-270, but this Constellation was used only for spares. Down in Chile a single Model L-049 was flown by Transportes Aereos Squella, this machine (c/n 2069) having the Chilean registration CC-CAA.

By the late 1970s the careers of a majority of the early generation Constellations (L-049 to 749A series) had ended even in Latin American countries, and it is believed the last of the type to be withdrawn from actual airline service was L-749A (c/n 2603). This aircraft operated with the Dominican Republic airline Aerolineas Argo SA (Argo SA) as HI-393 until it was grounded when the company ran into financial difficulties. This particular Constellation was still in perfect airworthy condition when impounded at Santa Dominga.

There were still two L-749A Constellations operational in Canada, however, during 1983: these belonged to Conifair Aviation Inc and they flew some 50hr per annum on anti-budworm spraying contracts during the two-month period when the budworm menace to trees was rife. The rest of the year was usually spent under wraps at their base near Montreal, the registrations of the two L-740As being C-GXKO (c/n 2601) and C-GXKR (c/n 2604).

Meanwhile in the United States itself, while TWA and Pan Am are regarded as having been the primary users of the early Constellations, the type was quite widely employed by several other American airline systems. One of the better known perhaps was Capital Airlines Inc, which was to be eventually taken over by United Airlines Inc on 1 June 1961. Capital Airlines was formed on 21 April 1948, having started life in 1936 as Pennsylvania Central Airlines Inc following a merger between Pennsylvania and Central Airlines. The company built up an expanding network of routes in the American eastern states and in the area of the Great Lakes, although there was a lack of long-haul services, with the exception of those to New Orleans and Florida. While employing a substantial number of British Vickers Viscounts (Model 745/700D) as well as DC-3s and 4s, Capital Airlines also acquired a number of Lockheed Constellations including 12 Model L-049s and seven L-749s, the 049s having fleet numbers from 750 to 761 inclusive, and the 749s 860 to 866 inclusive. In addition Capital purchased three 049s as reserve machines, these being registered as NC90827/28/29 (c/ns 1965, 1967 and 1968 respectively).

Another US company using Constellations was Capitol International Airways Inc of Nashville, Tennessee, which became one of America's major air charter airlines. At first they employed ex-USAF C-46 transports and DC-4s, but in 1957 took delivery of four Lockheed L-749As, these being registered N4900C (c/n 2663), N4901C (c/n 2671), N4902C (c/n 2566) and N9816F (c/n 2504).

Between 1946 and 1950, American Overseas Airlines Inc (AOA), later taken over by Pan Am,

Below:
This immaculate L-049A (c/n 2065) N86531 is seen here in 1965 as operated by Modern Air Transport. Originally with Capital Airlines (fleet No 750) it has been modified by having a nose extension to accommodate radar equipment. *MAP*

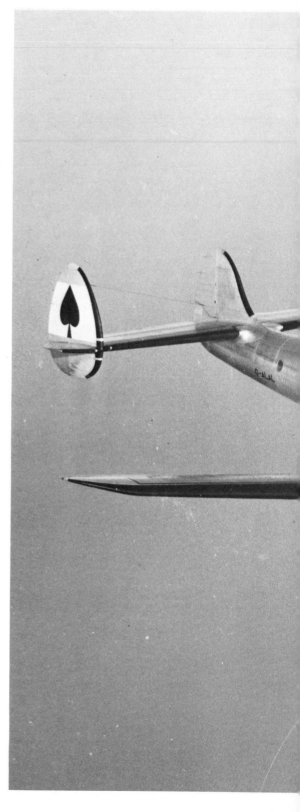

operated seven L-049 Constellations which carried
the registrations N90921 (c/n 2051), N90922
(c/n 2052), N90923 (c/n 2053), N90924 (c/n 2054),
N90925 (c/n 2063), N90926 (c/n 2064) and
N90927 (c/n 2065). Another company, American
Flyers Airline Corporation which was to merge with
Universal Airlines in 1971, also operated four L-049
Connies, two of which had previously been flown
by AOA. The four machines were : N90923
(c/n 2053), N88855 (c/n 2055), N90925 (c/n 2063)
and N88868 (c/n 2067). Miami-based ASA International Airlines employed three L-049s from 1962
to 1963, these being N86503 (c/n 2024), N86506
(c/n 2027) and N90926 (c/n 2064).

Another Miami-based concern, Associated Air
Transport Inc, flew four L-749A Constellations
during 1962-63, these being N103A (c/n 2520),
N117A (c/n 2614), N101A (c/n 2518) and N120A
(c/n 2617). From 1967 until 1969, a Texas-based
company known as Belizean Airlines operated one
L-049 (c/n 2068) registered as N8644, while a
decade earlier Braniff International Airways of
Dallas, Texas, was employing two L-049 Connies
registered N2520B (c/n 2081) and N2521B
(c/n 2082). Among other types, California Hawaiian
Airlines operated one L-049 and four L-749As
between 1952-62, the L-049 (c/n 1980) being
registered as N74192, while the L-749As
(c/ns 2519, 2521, 2610 and 2614) were registered
N102A, N104A, N115A and N117A respectively.

The L-749A Constellation also proved a popular
model with companies involved in firefighting and
anti-insect spraying activities, two American concerns being Aircraft Specialities Inc (later Globair
Inc) and Christler Flying Services Inc. In addition to
a fleet of Super Constellations, the first company
employed two L-749As registered as N608AS
(c/n 2600) and N611AS (c/n 2603), while the
Christler concern flew five L-749As (c/ns 2601,
2602, 2604, 2607 and 2609) registered N9464,
N9463, N9465, N9466 and N9467 respectively.

From 1958 until around 1962, the American
company known as Coastal Air Lines Inc operated a
small passenger-carrying fleet including four L-049
Connies registered N2737A (c/n 1976), N2740A
(c/n 1975), N67953 (c/n 1964) and N86532
(c/n 2069). During 1961-62 Great Lakes Airlines Inc
operated eight L-749A Constellations over its

Above:

At one time with KLM as PH-LKL, this L-1049G Super Connie (c/n 4840) is seen as N45516 when in service with the North Slope Supply Co, Anchorage, Alaska. *MAP*

routes, these aircraft comprising N102A (c/n 2519), N104A (c/n 2521), N105A (c/n 2522), N106A (c/n 2523), N107A (c/n 2524), N109A (c/n 2530), N115A (c/n 2610) and N117A (c/n 2614). Not surprisingly Howard Hughes of TWA fame operated four Constellations in one of his companies known as The Hughes Tool Co, these machines being three L-049s NC25600, N6000C and N6025C (c/ns 1961, 2070 and 2072) and L-749A N6025C (c/n 2671).

Numerous other small and independent airlines in the USA flew Constellations during a period lasting nearly three decades from the late 1940s until the 1970s. Among them was Imperial Airlines Inc which in 1961 operated three L-049s — N86532, N67953 and N2737A (c/ns 2069, 1964 and 1976 respectively); Intercontinental Airways from 1951 to 1953, four L-049s NC90827, NC90828 (later became NC67930), NC90829 and NC38936 (c/ns 1965, 1967, 1968 and 1962 respectively); Lloyd Airlines Inc, two L-049s N2520B and N2521B (c/ns 2081 and 2082 respectively) based in Miami in 1961; in the early 1960s two other Miami-based companies using Connies were Miami Airlines Inc, which operated four L-749As N9812F, N5595A, N9813F and N5596A (c/ns 2559, 2620, 2589 and 2619 respectively), and Magic City Airways, with two L-049s N86532 and N2521B (c/ns 2069 and 2082 respectively). Five L-049s were flown by McCulloch International Airlines Inc from 1964 until 1970,

these being N54214, N90823, N6000C, N90831 and N9412H (c/ns 1974, 2085, 2070, 1970 and 2072 respectively). From Trenton NJ and Miami, Modern Air Transport Inc operated a small fleet of Lockheed machines including five L-049s registered N86531, N86533, N67952, N2741A, N2739A (c/ns 2068, 2071, 1963, 1971 and 2065 respectively) and one L-749A N103A (c/n 2520).

California appears to have been a happy hunting ground for quite a number of early generation Constellations, for example Trans California Airlines operated a fleet of six L-749As in the mid-1960s, their registrations being N102A, N104A, N105A, N115A, N106A and N107A (c/ns 2519, 2521, 2522, 2610, 2523 and 2524 respectively); Transocean Airlines from Oakland flew four L-749As — N9816F, N9830F, N9812F and N9813F (c/ns 2504, 2551, 2559 and 2589 respectively), with one machine purchased apparently as a reserve, N2717A (c/n 2513). Also operating in California from 1968-70 were two

Constellations owned by Pacific Air Transport Inc, one L-049 N90816 (c/n 2078), the other being L-749A, N105A (c/n 2522), while from Burbank, Paradise Airlines flew three L-049s, N86504, N86506 and N9414H (c/n 2025, 2027 and 2075 respectively).

Three L-749As, registered N102A, N105A and N115A (c/ns 2519, 2522 and 2610 respectively) operated with Paramount Airlines of Burbank between 1961-62; also from Burbank, Schwimmer Aviation flew three L-049s from 1948 until 1967, these aircraft being NC90829, NC90827 and NC90828 (c/ns 1968, 1965 and 1967 respectively), with one machine (c/n 1962) bought for supplying spare parts only. Another California-based airline was Standard Airways Inc of San Diego, which from 1960 until 1964 operated a number of Lockheed types including three L-049s, N90831, N6000C and N86517 (c/ns 1970, 2070 and 2044 respectively), together with five L-749As registered N120A, N114A, N101A, N113A and N117A (c/ns 2617, 2535, 2518, 2534 and 2614 respectively).

Further north in the USA, the Model L-649A Constellation was favoured by Chicago and Southern Air Lines which between 1950 and 1953 operated six of the type registered N86521, N86522, N86523, N86524, N86525 and N86535 (c/ns 2642, 2653, 2659, 2660, 2662 and 2673 respectively), while a company named Dellair Inc flew three L-049s in 1964, these comprising N90831, N86517 and N6000C (c/ns 1970, 2044

Above:

Originally with TWA (fleet No 560), this L-049 (c/n 2078) N90816 is seen during 1966 when operating with Edde Airlines. Notice the elongated nose in which weather radar gear has been fitted.
MAP

and 2070 respectively). Other users of the Model L-049 in the USA are known to have included Edde Airlines Inc with N90816 (c/n 2078) and N9412H (c/n 2027); Futura Airlines Inc, N94144 (c/n 2075) and N86504 (c/n 2025); Hawthorne Nevada Airlines, N9412H (c/n 2072); Las Vegas Hacienda Inc, N9412H (c/n 2072), N90831 (c/n 1970), N9409H (c/n 2074) and N6000C (c/n 2070); World Wide Airlines Inc, N90831 (c/n 1970), N86517 (c/n 2044), N6000C (c/n 2070) and N9412H (c/n 2072); Trans American Aeronautical Corp, N2520B (c/n 2081), N2521B (c/n 2082), N67953 (c/n 1964) and N86532 (c/n 2069); International Caribbean Corp, N86533 (c/n 2071); Trans International Airlines Inc, N74192 (c/n 1980); US Airlines Inc, N74192 (c/n 1980) — leased 1951-52 from International Airlines Inc; Produce Custom Air Freight, N9412H (c/n 2072); Full Gospel Native Missionary Inc, N6000C (c/n 2070) and N90823 (c/n 2085); and John Ellis, who owned N86517 (c/n 2044) during 1967-68.

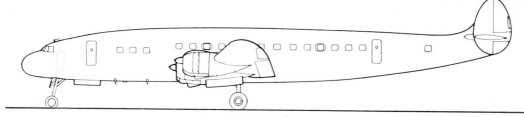

13 Old Connies Never Die . . .

Quite a number of Constellations continued operating in regular service into the late 1960s, for instance Pacific Northern Airlines Inc employed nine L-749As from 1955 until 1967, their registrations being N86523 (c/n 2659), N86524 (c/n 2660), N86525 (c/n 2662), N10401 (c/n 2661), N10403 (c/n 2622), N1593V (c/n 2556), N6017C (c/n 2655), N114A (c/n 2535) and N6022C (c/n 2668).

It will be noticed that a number of Constellations often changed hands, Pacific Northern's machines being no exception with five passing to Western Airlines Inc of Los Angeles in 1967. These were N6017C, N6022C, N1593V, N86524 and N86525; a sixth L-749A was added to Western's fleet, N1552V (c/n 2505). Initially N6017C, N6022C, N1552 and N1593V had Western fleet numbers 17C, 22C, 52V and 93V respectively, but these were altered to 517, 522, 552 and 593 in that order, while N86524 and N86525 were similarly fleet numbered 524 and 525.

World Wide Airlines Inc flew two L-749As — N4902C (c/n 2566) and N9812F (c/n 2559), while up north Wien Alaska Airlines Inc operated an L-749A registered N7777G (c/n 2553). Trans International Airlines Inc owned L-749A N4901C (c/n 2671), but this was normally leased out, as was N6021C (c/n 2667) another L-749A owned by Unlimited Leasing Inc from 1970 until 1979.

Although as far as is known it was not used on scheduled services, an L-749A flown by Las Vegas Hacienda was registered N120A (c/n 2617), and an ex-Western Airlines L-749A (c/n 2556) N1593V was purchased by a Claude R. Soto in 1969.

In England during 1961 Falcon Airways Ltd had bought three L-049 Constellations registered as G-AHEJ, G-AMUP and G-AHEL (c/ns 1975, 2051 and 1977 respectively), and in addition acquired

Below:
Initially in BOAC service, this L-049 Constellation (c/n 1977) G-AHEL is shown here during 1961 while operating with the British-owned Falcon Airways Ltd. *MAP*

another L-049 (c/n 1969) for Austria's Aero-Transport, registration OE-IFA.

Elsewhere a number of airlines also continued to fly L-749As on scheduled routes, although some were used purely as freighters especially when the new Super Constellations began to appear. Indeed some companies employed the Constellation purely as a freighter fleet, one example being the British-based Ace Freighters Ltd, which from 1964 onwards flew eight L-749As registered G-ANTF (c/n 2504), G-ASYS (c/n 2623), G-ASYF (c/n 2630), G-ASYT (c/n 2631), G-ASYU (c/n 2632), G-ALAK (c/n 2548), G-ALAL (c/n 2549) and G-ANUR (c/n 2565).

Meanwhile Ireland's national airline — Aerlinte Eireann (later Aer Lingus) had ordered five L-749As in 1947 for their intended transatlantic service to

Above:

These three L-749A Constellations are awaiting delivery in 1947 to Aerlinte Eireann (later Aer Lingus). They were sold to BOAC in 1948 after postponement of the Irish airline's transatlantic service to New York; c/ns were 2548 (EI-ACR), 2554 (EI-ADA) and 2549 (E1-ACS) believed to be nearest the camera. *Aer Lingus*

New York, these machines being delivered on 30 September that year. They were registered EI-ACR (c/n 2548), EI-ACS (c/n 2549), EI/ADA (c/n 2554), EI-ADD (c/n 2555) and EI-ADE (c/n 2566). The transatlantic service was temporarily abandoned, however, and after a short period of use on Dublin to Britain and continental routes the five L-749As were sold to BOAC in June 1948.

Austria's Aero-Transport flew two L-749As — OE-IFE/O (c/ns 2551 and 2562 respectively) — as well as L-049 OE-IFA (c/n 1969) from 1961 to 1964, another L-049, ex-G-AHEJ (c/n 1975) being used for spares.

Air Algerie operated four L-749As from 1955 to 1961, these being French registered F-BAZE/G/BDV/AZJ (c/ns 2624, 2626, 2677 and 2514 respectively), while Air Afrique flew one L-749A — F-BAZK (c/n 2515) — later registered CN-CCM (Morocco) — from 1961 onwards. In 1956 Air Ceylon ordered two L-749As (c/ns 2548 and 2549), but this lapsed although the company did fly PH-LDP (c/n 2638) leased from KLM, three more KLM L-749As joining this machine in 1957, these being PH-LDS/T/K (c/ns 2552, 2553 and 2590).

Air Inter of Paris operated three L-749As during 1961-62, all leased from Air France, these being F-BAZK/L/F (c/ns 2515, 2538 and 2625).

As mentioned elsewhere in this book, two L-749A 'tanker' Constellations were operating well into the early 1980s with the Canadian Conifair Aviation concern, but these machines (C-GXKO and C-GXKR) had previous to that flown with Beaver Air Spray when a third L-749A had accompanied them on similar operations, this machined being registered as C-GXKS (c/n 2609).

Meanwhile over in Africa, a Kenya-based company, Britair East Africa Ltd, operated an old Model L-049 (c/n 1977) during 1964-65, this

, machine being initially registered G-AHEL and later 5Y-ABF. Earlier in 1957, Ethiopian Airlines had purchased an L-749A (c/n 2608) registered as ET-T-35, but this aircraft lasted only about a month, entering service on 10 June and being written off after crashing in July. In 1962 a group of American businessmen formed the African airline known as Royal Air Burundi, the first aircraft purchased being a Lockheed L-049 Constellation (c/n 2072) carrying the registration N9412H. In Morocco RAM operated five L-749As between 1957 and 1970, the first machine CN-CCR (c/n 2512) arriving in October 1957, the next three during 1960 — CN-CCP, CN-CCN and CN-CCO (c/ns 2627, 2675, 2676 respectively) — and the fifth, CN-CCM (c/n 2515) in 1962. The four L-749As operated from 1950 onwards by SAA carried the registrations ZS-DBR/

Bottom:

Despite the appearance of more modern aircraft, a number of first generation Constellations were still in service with some of the major airlines during the late '50s and early '60s. This L-749 (c/n 2550) F-BAZP was still in Air France service in 1959. *MAP*

Below:

Minus its engines L-749A (c/n 2631) G-ASYT forlornly awaits the cutter's torch in 1966. It originally flew with South African Airways as ZS-DBT. *MAP*

DBS/DBT/DBU (c/ns 2623, 2630, 2631 and 2632 respectively), ZS-DBS and DBU operating later (1961-68) with South Africa's Trek Airways (Pty) Ltd. In North Africa, Tunis Air operated an L-749A from 1961, this machine being chartered from Air France and registered F-BAZO (c/n 2547).

A number of the early generation Constellations ended up as the sole representative of the type with some of the smaller concerns, or were often flown as a leased aircraft hired from a larger company, and some of those in this category not already mentioned are noted as follows: An L-049 (c/n 2036) owned by Cubana and registered CU-T547 was leased during 1957-59 to the Chilean company Sociedad de Transporte Aereos Ltda (ALA), which later became Cinta-Linea Aerea Chilena and was eventually absorbed by LADECO. During 1979 an airline known in the USA as Carib Airways Inc flew an L-749A registered as N6021C (c/n 2667), while earlier, between 1969-70, L-749A N6017C (c/n 2655) was owned by Vincent M. Castora, this machine being impounded in Panama City. From 1967 Central American Airways Flying Service Inc operated L-749A N273R (c/n 2650) for a number of years, and another American company CJS Aircargo Inc flew L-749A N7777G from 1970 until 1972. Another L-749A (c/n 2559) registered as N9812F and owned by Miami Airlines, was leased

during 1960 to Iceland's Loftleioir Creykjavik (Icelandic Airlines). A company concerned with anti-pest borate bombing, SS&T Aerial Contracting of Arizona, purchased an L-049 (c/n 2078) registered N90816 for this purpose in 1972, but it is believed this aircraft was not used and after about five years in storage was sold; an L-749A which was acquired and not believed to have been used belonged to Trans Bolivia Airlines of La Paz in 1968, this machine (c/n 2548) carrying the registration CP-797.

During 1964 the Luxembourg-based Interocean Airways SA operated one L-749A (c/n 2562) registered LX-10K, while earlier, from 1961 until 1962, the British-based Trans-European Airways had flown L-049 (c/n 1977) registered as G-AHEL.

This company had also ordered another L-049 (c/n 2036), G-ARHK, but this was never delivered although two other L-049s were on charge for spares, these being G-AHEJ and G-AMUP (c/ns 1975 and 2051 respectively).

One of the last European strongholds of the early generation Constellations in the mid-1960s was Great Britain, where Skyways of London Ltd were operating one L-149 and four L-749As as follows: the L-149 (c/n 1965) was registered as G-ARXE, the L-749As G-ALAK/AL/NUP/UR (c/ns 2548, 2549, 2562 and 2565 respectively). These aircraft were used mainly on freight services to the Far East as part of a contract for BOAC. Some of the last L-749As in regular American service also operated in freighter configuration, four of the type forming part of a cargo fleet which included a number of Super Constellations. The company owning these aircraft went under the name of Lance W. Dreyer and incorporated Transitional Cargo Inc, UNUM Inc, Air Cargo International Inc and Air International Inc. The group's four L-749As were N7777G

Below:
The L-749A Constellation (c/n 2553) residing at the Science Museum's Wroughton display. This picture was taken on 16 April 1979 and shows the aircraft prior to its timely rescue by 'Aces High' three years later. It stands here at Dublin Airport, where it had been since 1974 after flying a cattle ferry service between Ireland and Libya. *Roger P. Wasley*

(c/n 2553), N6021C (c/n 2667), N1206 (c/n 2613) and N86524 (c/n 2660).

By 1960, despite the appearance of more advanced types of aircraft, there was a surprising number of early generation Constellations still in service with some of the world's principal airlines including Air France (15), Braniff (2), Capital Airlines (11), Cubana (1), El-Al (1), KLM (10), Pacific Northern (6), Panair do Brasil (12), SAA (4) and Transocean (1). TWA, of course, still operated quite a number of its vast Constellation fleet at that time, the airline at one time owning 42 Model L-049s, 12 L-749s and 29 L-749As in addition to six C-69s which it flew as part of the USAAF Air Transport Command system.

There are not many Constellations extant in Europe today, but undoubtedly one of the finest examples is owned by the Science Museum and is housed at their site at Wroughton, Wiltshire. This particular aircraft has had a chequered career, originally going to KLM Royal Dutch Airlines in 1947 as PH-TET, its Lockheed c/n being 2553. Later it flew KLM's routes to Australia, Japan, South Africa and the United States until 1960, when it was replaced by KLM's new jet transport type the Douglas DC-8, and put into storage. After some three years the aircraft was sold to Wien Alaskan Airlines, converted to a mixed passenger/cargo configuration and allotted the US registration N7777G. From

1964 until 1966 it operated out of its base at Fairbanks, Alaska, before passing to several US-based companies including Lance W. Dreyer and CJS Aircargo Inc. In 1973, this L-749A was with Lanzair (CI) Ltd based in Jersey, Channel Islands, where it flew with the company's other L-749A (c/n 2650) registered N273R. During 1973 N7777G accompanied the Rolling Stones pop group on their tour of the Far East. The following year the aircraft began a cattle ferry service between Ireland and Libya, but after one trip it remained out of use at Dublin Airport. Thanks to a concern known as 'Aces High' and its managing director Mike Woodley, N7777G was rescued in 1982 after standing derelict at Dublin were it accumulated a pretty substantial 'parking fee' during seven years. This was also attended to by 'Aces High' who paid the fee to Aer Rianta, the Irish Airports Authority. At first it was hoped to have restored N7777G to airworthy condition and fly it across to England, but this plan was abandoned, and the aircraft had to be dismantled and conveyed by road to Dublin docks for the passage to Fleetwood, which was undertaken aboard the B&I Line vessel *Tipperary*. The L-749A had been given the British registration G-CONI, but for the Science Museum's Air Transport collection at Wroughton it has been repainted in its proper American colour scheme as a Constellation of TWA c1950-55, and has regained its original registration of N7777G. Now it is one of

the star attractions at Wroughton and it is planned to use it through 'Aces High' for demonstration purposes and possible filming.

Another well displayed L-749A can be seen in the Musée de l'Air in Paris, this being Lockheed c/n 2525, which originally went to Pan Am as N86527 before passing to Air France with whom it was registered F-BAZU. On completing its service with Air France, c/n 2525 flew as an engine test-bed, the powerplant on test being conveyed on a sturdy two-legged pylon on top of the fuselage. For this purpose the Connie was painted in a military colour scheme consisting of natural metal wings, lower fuselage, tailplane and rudders, orange-red fuselage cheat line sweeping back from nose to tail, with fins and wingtips the same orange-red and a white upper fuselage. French national roundels and fin flashes were carried and the registration F-ZVMV applied to the wings and fuselage sides.

Thus there are available on both sides of the Channel two fine examples of L-749A Constellations, aircraft representative of a type which did much to revolutionise world air travel after World War 2 and a class of aeroplane that gave reliable, speedy and comparatively comfortable service to many of the world's leading airlines until superseded by more modern types, among which was the Connie's illustrious successor the Super Connie and Starliner.

Left:
Unusual use of a Constellation was made in France with this L-749A (c/n 2525) which initially flew with Pan Am as N86527. It then went to Air France prior to becoming a flying test-bed for various engines. As can be seen here the powerplant was installed on a sturdy dorsal pylon to which was fitted an aerofoil section. The machine carried French military markings, but was allocated the civil registration F-ZVMV. *MAP*

Left:
Demise of a Connie: Baginton, Coventry, 11 October 1970. This picture tells the sad story of the end of a once beautiful aircraft. It was one of three sent to Baginton in the mid-1960s for spares: (c/n 2623) G-ASYS, (c/n 2631) G-ASYT and (c/n 2632) G-ASYU.
Roger P. Wasley

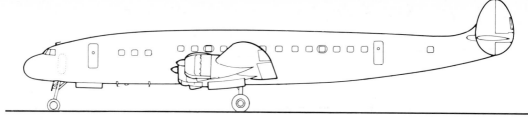

14 The Super Connie in Airline Service

While the early generation Constellations continued to provide excellent service with the various airlines both in the passenger-carrying and freighting role, it was not long before they were joined and eventually superseded by their larger brethren, Lockheed's Super Constellation — the L-1049 and subsequent series. As in the case of the earlier versions, TWA gave wholehearted support to the development of the Super Connie, but became in fact the second airline to receive the new type. EAL beat TWA to it, the first delivery from 14 L-1049s ordered arriving in time for Eastern to put the type into scheduled service of the New York to Miami route on 15 December 1951. These 14 Super Connies were registered N6201C-N6214C inclusive (c/ns 4001-4014) and given the EAL fleet Nos 201-214 respectively. It is interesting to observe that by the beginning of 1958, EAL had a total of 187 piston-engined airliners in its fleet for operating both long- and short-haul routes. These aircraft consisted of 56 Lockheed Constellations and Super Constellations, 46 of which were various versions of the Super Connie, seven DC-6Bs, 48 DC-7Bs, 20 Convair CV-440s and 56 Martin 4-0-4s. It was also EAL which, in April 1961, inaugurated the world's first guaranteed seat service with no reservation required, this 'air shuttle' starting with EAL's Super Constellations.

There were 24 Model L-1049s built, and the remaining 10 machines went to TWA so that on 10 September 1952 the airline was able to commence its New York to Los Angeles service. These 10 L-1049s were registered N6901C-N6910C inclusive (c/ns 4015-4024) and carried the TWA fleet Nos 901-910 respectively. With the introduction of the updated L-1049C Super Connie, the first of which made its initial flight on 17 February 1953, those airlines ordering the type would be assured of an improved performance over the preceding L-1049 model by way of the more powerful Wright Turbo-Compound engines

and higher take-off weight. The first L-1049C (c/n 4501) was delivered to KLM Royal Dutch Airlines on 10 June 1953 registered as PH-TFP; on 15 August the same year it entered service on KLM's nonstop New York to Amsterdam route, although a refuelling stop was made on the return flight from Amsterdam to New York at either Prestwick or Shannon. This was normal procedure in those days for westbound transatlantic airliners because of the prevailing Atlantic headwinds usually encountered. Other KLM long-distance routes served Australia, South Africa and South America, and to operate these services KLM, in addition to PH-TFP and a number of DC-6s and DC-6Bs, acquired a further 12 L-1049Cs for the fleet. The first eight machines were initially registered as PH-TFR/TFS/TFT/TFU/TFV/TFW/TFX/TFY (c/ns 4502-4509 respectively), but later these registrations were changed to PH-LKR/LKS/LKT/LKU/LKV/LKW/LKX/LKY respectively, with the original PH-TFP becoming PH-LKP. The remaining four L-1049Cs when delivered had the registrations PH-LKA/LKB/LKC/LKD (c/ns 4553, 4558, 4559 and 4560 respectively).

On 19 October 1953 TWA put the L-1049C Super Constellation into service on its Ambassador route between Los Angeles and New York, this being the first regular scheduled nonstop transcontinental run on a coast-to-coast basis. Seven L-1049C Super Constellations from the last 11 built went to TWA (c/ns 4550, 4551, 4552, 4554, 4555, 4557 and 4558), the other four going to KLM including c/n 4560, which was the final L-1049C produced before the first L-1049E (c/n 4561) commenced building, although most L-1049Es emerged as L-1049Gs off the assembly lines.

In addition to its fleet of 17 L-1049s and L-1049Cs, TWA was to purchase a further 38 Super Constellations comprising 29 of the more advanced L-1049G (Super 'G') model and nine L-1049Hs, the dual-purpose passenger/freight variant. During

1956 Super Connies enabled TWA to inaugurate a transatlantic two-class passenger service (first class and tourist), and in the following year transpolar routes were opened by TWA between Los Angeles and London via San Francisco, and to Paris and Rome.

Although the L-1049C production programme was intended primarily to supply TWA and KLM with the type, other international airlines began sending in orders and in the event 60 L-1049Cs were produced. Of these, in addition to the 13 and seven supplied to KLM and TWA respectively, 10 went to Air France registered as F-BGNA/B/C/D/E/F/G/H/I/J (c/ns 4510-4519 respectively); two to Air India as VT-DGL/M (c/ns 4547 and 4548); 16 to Eastern Air Lines Inc registered as N6215C/16C/17C/18C/19C/20C/21C/22C/23C/24C/25C/26C/27C/28C/29C/30C (c/ns 4523-4538 respectively), the EAL fleet numbers corresponding accordingly from 215 to 230 inclusive. Three flew with Pakistan International Airlines registered AP-AFQ/R/S (c/ns 4520, 4521 and 4522 respectively); four were delivered to QANTAS as

Above:
This L-1049C Super Constellation (c/n 4553) is in Air Ceylon livery and registered 4R-ACH. It was, however, owned by KLM initially as PH-LKA, who leased it to Air Ceylon in 1959. *MAP*

VH-EAG/H/I/J (c/ns 4539, 4545, 4546 and 4549 respectively) and another five L-1049Cs went to Trans-Canada Air Lines as CF-TGA/B/C/D/E (c/ns 4540, 4541, 4542, 4543 and 4544 respectively), the corresponding TCA fleet numbers being 401, 402, 403, 404 and 405 accordingly. As with the earlier Constellations, quite a number of

Below:
In landing configuration is KLM's PH-LKL, an L-1049H (c/n 4840), which also operated with Flying Tiger Line (fleet No 818), World Airways Inc, Lance W. Dreyer, North Slope Supply Co of Anchorage, Alaska, and Globair. *MAP*

Top:
The beautiful lines of the Super Constellation are captured well in this picture of Air India International's L-1049C (c/n 4547) VT-DGL, *Rani of Jhansi.* *Air India*

Above:
Standing at Miami International Airport in 1978, Lockheed L-1049C (c/n 4532) N6224C at one time operated with Eastern Air Lines as fleet No 224.
Roger P. Wasley

the Super Connies changed hands as more modern types of aircraft entered service with the major airlines, and several c/ns and registrations will be found under the banner of a number of secondary airlines.

Air France, which was formed way back in August 1933 with the merger of four airlines — Air Union, Farman, CIDNA and Air Orient — expanded rapidly until the time of World War 2 when those machines that could be salvaged from the Air France fleet went to North Africa to support the Allies. On 26 June 1945 the French civil aviation industry was nationalised and Air France changed from being a private company to that of a state enterprise. Expansion followed the war and much-needed new equipment like the Lockheed Constellation and Super Constellation began to arrive to supplement the DC-3s and DC-4s. By 1950 Air France was carrying three times as many passengers as had been carried by French airlines in the 20-year period before the war. Scheduled services to Montreal were inaugurated on 20 October that year and on 27 April 1952 the first service to Mexico was started. By 1954 Air France was operating, along with its other aircraft types, 21 L749/749A Constellations and 10 Super Connies, thus enabling the airline to further develop its international routes. By 1958 it was flying the polar route to Japan and China via Anchorage, Alaska (starting on 10 April) and to Moscow, inaugurated in

August that year. Although 6 May 1959 saw the introduction of the French-built jet Caravelle airliner into Air France service on the Paris to Istanbul route via Rome and Athens, the fleet by then was accounted for mostly by Lockheed types including 15 Constellations, 22 Super Constellations and 10 of the new L-1649A Starliners. By the early part of 1960, however, with the introduction of Boeing 707 jets, the 40-year period of French piston-engined civil aviation was drawing to a close. Most of the Lockheed aircraft were disposed of, although in the early 1960s when Max Bruch was Air France's manager in the Far East, Super 'G' Constellations were operating the Paris to Far East service four times a week. Following their L-1049C order, Air France had in fact contracted for 14 Super 'G' Constellations and these were delivered as F-BHBA/B/C/D/E/F/G/H/I/J (c/ns 4620-4727/ 4634 and 4639 respectively) and F-BHMI/J/K/L (c/ns 4668-4671 respectively).

Meanwhile Air India, as mentioned earlier, had received two L-1049C Super Connies and an order for a further eight machines was placed, these arriving in Bombay as three Model L-1049Es registered VT-DHL/M/N (c/ns 4613-4615) and five L-1049Gs — VT-DIL/M/N/DJW/X (c/ns 4646, 4666, 4667, 4686 and 4687 respectively). These Super Connies of Air India (which had changed its name from Air India International on 8 June 1962) enabled the state-owned airline to open new routes

Above left:
Air France continued to put its faith in the Constellation design by ordering Super Connies. This Super 'G' (c/n 4634) F-BHBI taxies past the camera in the summer of 1966. *MAP*

Left:
This Super 'G' (c/n 4671) is an ex-Air France machine. It is shown here in the colours of Compagnie Air Fret bearing the same French registration — F-BHML. In 1960 this aircraft was chartered to Tunis Air. *MAP*

in an easterly direction taking in Singapore (via Madras), Bangkok, Hong Kong, Tokyo, Darwin and Sydney. Tashkent and Moscow were added to Air India's list of destinations from April 1959 by which time the airline's route lengths had increased to some 19,000 miles.

On 7 June 1954 Pakistan International Airlines Corporation (PIA) started operating its first three L-1049C Super Constellations (mentioned earlier) over the route between Karachi (West Pakistan) and Dacca (East Pakistan) — now Bangladesh. PIA, however, really came into its own after 11 March 1955 when it merged with Orient Airways Ltd, which until then had been the major domestic operator within Pakistan. Thus PIA became an autonomous corporation which, as well as serving East and West Pakistan, flew to the Middle East, India, Burma and Europe. For these services, in addition to its L-1049Cs, Vickers Viscounts and DC-3s, PIA acquired two more Super Constellations, these being L-1094Hs, the convertible passenger/cargo carrying variant, which were registered AP-AJY/Z (c/ns 4835 and 4836).

The success of the early variants of the Super Constellation persuaded well over a dozen of the world's airlines to choose the Super 'G' model as it became available with its uprated Turbo-Compound DA3s and tip tanks giving improved performance and a much longer range.

For example, the Australian airline QANTAS (the initials derive from the original company of the 1920s, Queensland and Northern Territory Aerial Services Ltd, to which 'Empire Airways' was added in 1934) further added to its Super Connie fleet by ordering 10 L-1049Gs and two L-1049Hs. QANTAS was a very enthusiastic user of the Connie and Super Connie, and indeed this faith in the type was exemplified on 29 March 1954: that day at Lockheed's Burbank plant, Lady Spender, wife of the Australian Ambassador to the USA, took part in a special ceremony to christen the first QANTAS L-1049C Super Constellation named *Southern Constellation*, VH-EAG (c/n 4539). Instead of a bottle of champagne being used to break over the nose of the aircraft, a pan of gold-bearing sand taken from the goldfields of both Australia and California was tipped on to it, this symbolising the first link between these regions during the gold-rush days a century earlier.

With the advent of the Super Connies, QANTAS was enabled to open up new services to the North American continent, with transatlantic flights commencing on 15 May 1954. Twice a week there was a service from Sydney to San Francisco or Vancouver via Fiji, Canton Island and Hawaii. In 1956, when Australia was host to the XVIth Olympic Games at Melbourne, QANTAS carried record traffic on all its routes, and in addition to scheduled services no less than 70 special Olympic Games flights were undertaken. During that time on more than a dozen occasions, QANTAS had its entire Super Constellation fleet in the air at the same time, a fitting tribute not only to the aircraft itself, but also to the efficiency of the engineering and maintenance staff of QANTAS. The airline also flew the Olympic Flame in a Super Connie from Athens to Darwin, a flight of some 8,600 miles, the longest journey ever made with the Flame and the first time it had crossed the Equator to the Southern Hemisphere.

After an agreement between Australia and the USA in which permission was granted for QANTAS to operate across the United States through San Francisco and New York, before flying on across the Atlantic to Great Britain and Europe, QANTAS put into operation its round-the-world service. This was the first of its kind, and was inaugurated on 14 January 1958 with two Super 'G' Constellations

Left:
A QANTAS Super Constellation in full cry: this is L-1049G (c/n 4679) VH-EAO, Southern Aurora. *QANTAS*

— VH-EAO *Southern Aurora* (c/n 4679) and VH-EAP *Southern Zephyr* (c/n 4680). The two aircraft took off from Melbourne and flew to Sydney where they parted company, one flying west along the 'Kangaroo' route to London via the Middle East, while the second machine flew east across the Pacific to San Francisco, New York and thence to London. It was not long after this that eight round-the-world services a week were being operated, four by QANTAS and four in association with BOAC. It is interesting to note that VH-EAO was returned to Lockheed's as N9722C on 14 October 1959, having been acquired two years earlier on 28 October 1957. However, less than a year later on 18 August 1960, this Super 'G' was returned to QANTAS and re-registered as VH-EAO, but its name was changed appropriately to *Southern Prodigal* and it remained with QANTAS for nearly three years before returning to the USA after being sold to Calif Airmotive.

Super Constellations allowed QANTAS to make the flying kangaroo emblem familiar in 23 countries on five continents around the world, and by December 1958 QANTAS had increased its international network to some 72,725 miles. Just one QANTAS Super Connie was involved in an accident when, on 24 August 1960, VH-EAC *Southern Wave* (c/n 4606) crashed while taking-off from Mauritius fortunately without any fatal casualties, but the aircraft itself was a write-off.

As for the two L-1049H Super Connies operated by QANTAS, the first, VH-EAM *Southern Spray* (c/n 4801), was the subject of a special christening ceremony in October 1956 to celebrate the type's dual role. This occasion was intended to highlight the L-1049H variant's purpose as a passenger/ cargo aircraft and was performed by two Australian girls — Lola Fry and Pamela Cooke — who stood one each side of the Super Constellation's nose on raised platforms and broke a traditional bottle of champagne each on the port and starboard sides. The two L-1049Hs were quickly put into service during 1956 to assist with the QANTAS Pacific service involved in the Olympic Games traffic.

With the entry into QANTAS service of the Boeing 707s, the airline's Super Connies were relegated to more mundane duties like freighting, but even this fell off as extra cargo space became available on the big jets. Even so in 1959 the two L-1049Hs became involved in a massive airlift when they flew from the United States to Australia transporting 46,000lb of components required for the Boeing simulator which QANTAS had acquired.

Meanwhile Trans-Canada Air Lines added another nine Lockheed Super Constellations to its fleet of five L-1049Cs already mentioned. The nine comprised three L-1049Es registered CF-TGF/G/H (c/ns 4563, 4564 and 4565), four L-1049Gs — CF-TEU/V/W/X (c/ns 4641, 4643, 4682 and 4683 respectively) and two L-1049Hs registered CF-TEY/Z (c/ns 4850 and 4851). These aircraft, together with the original five TCA L-1049Cs, were employed from 14 May 1954 on the airline's transatlantic routes, while from the following 26 September the Super Connies replaced the TCA North Stars on Canadian transcontinental services. By the end of 1957 Trans-Canada's Super 'G' Connies were flying a nonstop route across the Atlantic to London, Paris and Düsseldorf.

Below:
Viewed from another machine, QANTAS Super 'G' (c/n 4607) VH-EAD *Southern Dawn*, flies low across a part of its Australian homeland. *QANTAS*

Left:
**An unidentified
Trans-Canada (now
Air Canada) L-1049C
Super Constellation
about to land at
London Airport in the
1950s.**
TCA/Air Canada

A Trans-Canada Airline's Super Constellation

Above:
Trans-Canada Airlines operated this Super Connie until 1962. An L-1049H (c/n 4850), it was registered CF-TEY, fleet No 413, but in this picture taken later in its career it is with Central American Airways as N74CA. *MAP*

Below:
A Lufthansa Super 'G', (c/n 4604) D-ALIN, on public display in 1985. *MAP*

In West Germany Deutsche Lufthansa, which had been forced to close down as Deutsche Luft Hansa in 1945, was re-formed in 1953 as Luftag but changed its name to Deutsche Lufthansa AG on 6 August 1954 and awaited the arrival of its first four Lockheed L-1049Gs. These Super 'G' Connies were registered D-ALAK/EM/IN/OP (c/ns 4602-4605 respectively) and soon entered service on Lufthansa's Hamburg to New York service via Düsseldorf and Shannon beginning on 8 June 1955, with more cities on the North Atlantic route being added which included a direct service between Manchester and Chicago commencing on 23 April 1956. The following August a new route was opened between West Germany and Argentina (Buenos Aires), which in May 1958 was extended to Santiago.

By now Lufthansa had ordered four more Super 'G' Constellations which were registered D-ALAP/ EC/OF/ID (c/ns 4637, 4640, 4642 and 4647 respectively), these supplementing the original four on the airline's long-distance routes, which now included the Middle East — commenced September 1956 — while later a route to Bangkok was started during November 1959, by which time four L-1649A Starliners had also joined the Lufthansa fleet. It is also believed that two L-1049Hs were put into service, but as the only registrations traced for these are N1880 and N6921C (c/ns 4820 and 4817) they may have only been leased. It is known that during 1962-63 Lufthansa did lease out some of its L-1049Gs to the Italian airline Alitalia, these flying mostly on charter flights.

The Spanish airline Lineas Aereas de Espana SA (IBERIA) used a number of Super Constellations starting with three Model L-1049Cs registered EC-AIN/O/P (c/ns 4550-4552), fleet Nos 201/2/3, these being acquired in 1954 and opening up the airline's service to New York in September of that year. Routes were extended to cover several European countries, North and South America and Africa and it was necessary to order more aircraft, IBERIA contracting for five L-1049Gs and an extra L-1049C. The Super 'G' Connies were registered EC-AMP/Q/QM/QN/RN (c/ns 4673, 4676, 4644, 4645 and 4678 respectively), the L-1049C being EC-AQL (c/n 4553).

Top:
This fine in-flight study is of Lufthansa's L-1049G Super Connie D-ALAP (c/n 4637) and shows off the superb lines of the aircraft to perfection. *Lufthansa*

Above:
An L-1049C Super Constellation of the Spanish airline Iberia stands at its dispersal point. Registered EC-AIN, this machine (c/n 4550) carried the Iberian fleet No 201. *MAP*

15 Super Connies and Starliners in the Jet Age

By the beginning of the 1980s there were around 10 Lockheed Constellations and Super Constellations remaining in airline service, mostly in South America. The decline in the operational status of this once magnificent aircraft had been a slow process however, and really began in the late 1950s with the introduction into service by the major airlines of the big jet-liners like the Boeing 707 and Douglas DC-8. Consequently the larger companies started selling off their surplus piston-engined types so that machines in the Douglas DC-4, 6 and 7 series, together with numerous variants of the Constellation and Super Constellation, became readily available to smaller airline operators around the world.

In the case of the Super Constellations, like the Constellation variants before them, many were acquired both for passenger-carrying and freighting in Latin American countries. The Colombian airline AVIANCA acquired four Super Constellations in addition to their six L-749As, the Super Connies consisting of three L-1049Cs registered HK-175/176/177 (c/ns 4554, 4555 and 4556 respectively)

and one L-1049G as HK-184 (c/n 4628). This airline ran a transatlantic service to Lisbon, Madrid, Paris, Rome and later to Hamburg and Frankfurt, while a South American transcontinental flight to Lima, Peru, was started on 1 June 1957. Cuba's airline Cubana began using an L-1049C from 22 November 1954 on its services to Madrid and Mexico City, this aircraft — CU-P-573 (c/n 4557) — being later supplemented by three L-1049Gs registered CU-T-601/602/631 (c/ns 4632, 4633 and 4675 respectively), which from 12 May 1956 operated a daily nonstop service between Havana and New York. One of the Super 'G's was usually leased to Chile's airline Sociedad de Transportes Aereos Ltda (ALA) when its L-049 was undergoing overhaul.

Below:
Although registered here as N1005C, this L-1049C Super Constellation (c/n 4557) also operated at one time with Cubana as CU-P-573. *MAP*

The Mexican airline Aerovias Guest, in which the controlling interest had been bought by the Scandinavian Airline System (SAS) on 20 February 1959, added three Super 'G' Connies to its L-749A fleet, these L-1049Gs — XA-NAC/NAD/NAF (c/ns 4672, 4677 and 4678 respectively) — being employed on the airline's Atlantic, Central American, Caribbean and Miami services.

In Venezuela, Linea Aeropostal Venezolana (LAV), which had first started a service to New York with Constellations on 12 March 1947, added eight Super Constellations to its fleet between 1954-56. These machines consisted of two L-1049Es, YV-C-AMR (re-registered AMS) named *Rafael Urdaneia* (c/n 4561) and YV-C-AMT (later rebuilt as L-1049G and registered YV-C-ANF) named *Simon Bolivar* (c/n 4562), plus six L-1049Gs registered YV-C-AME/AMI/ANB/ANC/AND/ANE (c/ns 4636, 4674, 4572, 4575, 4576 and 4577 respectively).

The Brazilian airline Redes Estaduais Aereas Limitida (REAL) acquired three convertible passenger/cargo L-1049H Super Connies during February 1958, and these inaugurated a new service by REAL to Los Angeles via Manaus, Bogota and Mexico City commencing in November 1959. Another L-1049H was added to the fleet, and on 9 July 1960 the service was extended to include a transpacific route to Tokyo calling at Honolulu. The four L-1049Hs, which later went to VARIG of Brazil, were registered PP-YSA/B/C/D (c/ns 4833, 4834, 4837 and 4838 respectively), the same registrations applying to both airlines.

Empresa de Viacao Aerea Rio Grandense SA (VARIG) had been told in February 1953 by the Brazilian Government it could fly the new Brazil to New York route, and an order was immediately placed for three L-1049E Super Constellations (c/ns 4582, 4583 and 4584) to be allotted the registrations PP-VDA/B/C, but this was changed to an order for three L-1049Gs which were then becoming available. On arrival at Rio de Janeiro the

first three Super 'G' Connies (c/ns 4610, 4611 and 4612) retained the registrations intended for the L-1049Es, and on 2 August 1955 VARIG's service to New York via Belem, Port of Spain, and Ciudad Trujillo (Dominican Republic) was inaugurated. In November that year VARIG was able to extend its route mileage by starting a service to Buenos Aires, and purchased a further three L-1049Gs registered PP-VDD/E/F (c/ns 4681, 4684 and 4685) as well as the four L-1049Hs from REAL mentioned earlier.

Other Latin American operators known to have used Super Connies include: Aeromar, Dominican Republic, which leased L-1049H N1007C (c/n 4805) from Air Cargo Support from 1977-79; Aerotours Dominicano, L-1049 HI-228 (c/n 4009) and L-1049C HI-329 (c/n 4536) from 1974-79; Aerotransportes Entre Rios SRL, Argentina, L-1049G LV-IXZ (c/n 4580) and L-1049Hs LV-PJU (later JHF)/J10/PKW (later JJO), (c/ns 4801, 4808 and 4807 respectively); Aerovias, Panama, L-1049Gs HP-280/281 (c/ns 4677 and 4678); AFISA, Panama, L-1049H N6917C/HP-526 (c/n 4815); Aviateca, Guatemala, L-1049H N6932C (c/n 4823); Bolivian International Airways, L-1049H CP-998 (c/n 4805); CAUSA, Uruguay, L-1049H CX-BEM (c/n 4818); LEBCA, Venezuela, L-1049Hs YV-C-LBP/LBI (c/ns 4807, 4808); Lineas Aereas Patagonias Argentinas SRL, L-1049H LV-ILW (c/n 4166); RAPSA, Panama, L-1049C HP-475 (c/n 4551 ex-TWA) and L-1049G HP-467 (c/n 4678); TABSA, Bolivia, L-1049Hs (c/ns 4807 and 4801) registered CP-797 in both cases, also operated L-1049G (c/n 4581) known to have at one time been registered N442LM; Transcontinental

Below:

In this picture L-1049C (c/n 4557), which flew with Cubana as CU-P-573, is seen when serving with Capitol Airways during 1967 registered N1005C.
MAP

Wings excepted, the similarity between the L-1049G/H Super Connie and the L-1649A Starliner are apparent here. This machine, (c/n 4843) N45515, was an L-1049H and had long since ceased flying when this picture was taken at Kingman in

November 1976. At one time it flew as PH-LKN with KLM, and after several changes of ownership ended up with Globair with whom it flew in the role of crop sprayer and anti-fire borate bomber.
Roger P. Wasley

SA, Argentina, which started a Buenos Aires to New York service in September 1958, with L-1049Hs LV-FTU/FTV (c/ns 4846 and 4847); and VIASA, Venezuela, which in 1961 was operating one L-1049E YV-C-ANF (c/n 4562) and two L-1049Gs YC-C-AME/AMI (c/ns 4636 and 4674 respectively).

The numbers of Super Constellations made redundant by the big airlines as the jets moved in were bought up quickly by numerous companies — from those running a substantial fleet of aircraft to one-plane operators. In the United States alone over 60 concerns became Super Connie operators and exceeded the number of users in Latin American countries. Also many 'second-hand' Super Constellations went to secondary airlines in the Middle and Far East, Africa and New Zealand, where they flew in both passenger and cargo configuration.

As there were comparatively few European operators of the Super Constellation, they can be dealt with in a little more detail. The Irish international airline Aer Lingus for example, started its Dublin to New York service on 28 April 1958 with an L-1049C leased from America's Seaboard and Western airline. This machine, registered N1005C (c/n 4557), was joined later by a Super 'G', N611C (c/n 4602) and two L-1049Hs registered as N1008C (c/n 4806) and N1009C (c/n 4807), these four Super Connies flying with

Aer Lingus until early in 1961 when they were superseded by Boeing 720-048 jets.

Apart from Air France, two other French operators of Super Constellations were Air Fret and Catair, both of whom flew a mixed L-1049C and Super 'G' fleet. In the case of Air Fret one L-1049C, registered F-BRAD (c/n 4519) operated alongside three Super 'G's — F-BHBB/BI/ML (c/ns 4621, 4634 and 4671), all four aircraft being ex-Air France machines. The Air Fret L-1049C also flew with Catair, a company that had three other L-1049Cs in its fleet, these being F-BGNC/NH/NG (c/ns 4512, 4513 and 4516 respectively), as well as two Super 'G's registered F-BHBE/MI (c/ns 4624 and 4668).

Another European operator, Lanzair (CI) Ltd of Jersey in the Channel Islands, flew a single Super 'G' in the mid-1970s — N11SR (c/n 4581); in Spain, Inter-City Airways (Madrid) operated L-1049H N469C (c/n 4847) during 1968, both apparently leased machines.

America's Seaboard and Western airline leased three of their L-1049H Super Constellations to the Belgian airline SABENA in the late 1950s, these machines being registered N1006C/7C/8C (c/ns 4802, 4805 and 4806), while in France SAFA of Paris chartered its Super 'G' Connies from Air France.

Down in Portugal, Transportes Aereos Portugueses (TAP) had taken delivery of its first L-1049G

Top:
In full Aerlinte Eireann (later Aer Lingus) livery, L-1049C Super Constellation (c/n 4557) N1005C stands outside Dublin Airport departure terminal. This machine was leased to the Irish airline by Seaboard and Western Airlines of the USA between 1958 and 1960. *Aer Lingus*

Above:
Transportes Aereos Portugueses (TAP) employed Super Constellations on its international routes. Pictured in 1967 is Super 'G' (c/n 4616). *MAP*

CS-TLA (c/n 4616), on 15 July 1955, this aircraft being named *Vasco da Gama* and entering service on TAP's European routes as well as those to Luanda and Lourenco Marques in Mozambique. It was later joined in TAP service by four more Super 'G's and one L-1049H, the L-1049Gs being registered CS-TLB/C/E/F (c/ns 4617, 4618, 4677 and 4672 respectively) and the L-1049H CS-TLD (c/n 4808).

In the meantime Pan Am were flying their nonstop transatlantic service with Douglas DC-7s, and TWA having persuaded Lockheed to evolve the L-1649A Starliner from the Super 'G' as a rival contender to Pan Am on the Atlantic route, introduced this ultimate Constellation variant on their New York-London-Paris service on 1 June 1957. Naming this latest acquisition from Lockheed as the 'Jetstream', TWA purchased 29 of the type but they did not last long in the airline's service; the jet era had already started, sounding the death knell for piston-engined airliners in major airline service. Indeed of those L-1649As used by TWA at least 12 flew as pure freighters with the company from 1960 onwards.

Air France ordered 10 L-1649A Starliners from Lockheed which were entered on the French register as F-BHBK/L/M/N/O/P/Q/R/S/T (c/ns 1011, 1020, 1027, 1028, 1031, 1032, 1033, 1036, 1044 and 1045 respectively). The West German airline Lufthansa purchased four Starliners registered D-ALUB/AN/ER/OL (c/ns 1034, 1040, 1041 and 1042 respectively), of which two were employed as freighters. Two of Lufthansa's Starliners (c/ns 1041 and 1042) also operated with Condor Flugdienst during the period 1960-62 carrying the same registrations, which was not surprising as this company was actually a subsidiary of Lufthansa at that time.

The South African company Trek Airways (Pty) Ltd owned the same two L-1649As mentioned above in due course when they were initially registered ZS-DTM (c/n 1041) and ZS-DVJ (c/n 1042). However, they flew in the colours of Luxembourg's Luxair airline between 1964-69 although still owned by Trek, and were joined by another Starliner registered LX-LGY (c/n 1036), the original two machines being LX-LGX/Z (1042 and 1041 respectively) when with Luxair.

Meanwhile in the United States, from their Oakland, California, base, World Airways Inc flew four L-1649As which they had added to their Super Constellation fleet. These Starliners were US registered as N45511/12/17/20 (c/ns 1034, 1040, 1041 and 1042), and as can be seen our old friends 1041 and 1042 have turned up again, which is a good example of how the Starliners that were available (only 43 were built) changed hands, as had the earlier families of Constellations and Super Connies. One Starliner was operated by a religious/political organisation calling itself Moral

Right:
In the colours of Transportes Aereos Portugueses (TAP) in 1959, this L-1049H (c/n 4808) CC-TLD flew later with LEBCA (Linea Expresa Bolivar Compania Anomina) of Venezuela, when it was allotted the registration YV-C-LBI. *MAP*

Right:
Much leasing out was done by companies owning Super Constellations, an example being this L-1049H (c/n 4808) N1010C in Seaboard and Western livery, but leased by EAL. Likewise Seaboard and Western leased quite a number of their aircraft to other international operators. *MAP*

Top left: **A Transportes Aereos Portugueses (TAP) L-1049G (c/n 4617) CS-TLB is seen taxying at Heathrow on a wet and misty day in 1958.** *MAP*

Centre left: **Super Connie L-1049H (c/n 4819) is shown in Amco International livery during 1969. Registered N6919C it was on lease from Murphree Air International, but its main operational career had been with the Flying Tiger Line (fleet No 809) as a freighter.** *MAP*

Below: **Air France, following its traditional investment in the Constellation family, introduced 10 L-1649A Starliners into its fleet. This one, (c/n 1011) F-BHBK, demonstrates admirably the combination of the sleek Connie fuselage and 150ft span laminar flow wing.** *Lockheed*

Overleaf: **Lufthansa's L-1649A Starliner D-ALUB (c/n 1034) roars past with its four 3,400hp R-3350-EA2 Turbo-Compound radials in fine tune.** *Lockheed*

Rearmament Corporation during 1964-65, this aircraft being registered N7314C (c/n 1016) and originally belonging to TWA. Another one L-1649A was N974R (c/n 1040), initially owned by World Airways as N45512, but operating during 1976-77 with Proimex International of Denver, Colorado, as a freighter.

Up in Alaska during 1968-69 the Prudhoe Bay Oil Distributing Co flew three Starliners as pure cargo-carriers, these aircraft being N7315C, N7316C and N8083H (c/ns 1017, 1018 and 1038 respectively). Trans American Leasing Inc of Miami acquired three Starliners for use in the 1968-73 period, these having the registrations N7311C/ 22C/24C (c/ns 1013, 1025 and 1030).

CJS Aircargo flew our familiar c/n 1040 for a two-year period (1970-72) still registered as N974R, the Hughes Tool Co operated one L-1649A — N7310C (c/n 1012) — while Lockheed themselves used c/n 1001 which flew with three different registrations over a period of time, these being N1649, N90968 and N1102. An airline known as Starflite Inc flew a number of Starliners during the mid-1960s, but no other details of these are known at the time of writing, while from Bethel in Alaska, West-Air Inc operated three L-1649As and held two for spares. The operational machines were N7316C, N8083H and N974R (c/ns 1018, 1038 and 1040), while the remaining two were N7315C and N7312C (c/ns 1017 and 1024). It will be noticed all these changed hands several times on perusal of the above summary including, yet again, c/n 1040 still as N974R.

There seems little doubt that had the turbojet transports not developed so quickly into a very economical proposition for the long-haul international airlines, the Lockheed Starliner would have, like the Connie and Super Connie before it, proved a world winner. But fate in the shape of progress decreed otherwise, and with only just over 40 L-1649As ordered, Lockheed was unable to recover in sales the cost of introducing the Starliner. Nevertheless this aesthetically pleasing aeroplane was without a doubt the piston-engined airliner taken to the peak of its proficiency. It was the last in a line of magnificent four-engined airliners by Lockheed that had started back in the mid-1940s when America was at war and ironically, although the Starliners had been withdrawn by the 1960s from the fleets of primary users, some of the original old Constellations still plodded on for a number of years around Latin America right into the 1970s, a fitting tribute to what has come to be regarded as a classic among the world's greatest civil aircraft.

Right:
Sadly this was the fate of many Super Constellations. Here N6227C (c/n 4535) is pictured in its final days at Miami International Airport during March 1978. It had started out with Eastern Air Lines (fleet No 227) and is believed to have finished up with Proimex International Ltd of Denver, Colorado. *Roger P. Wasley*

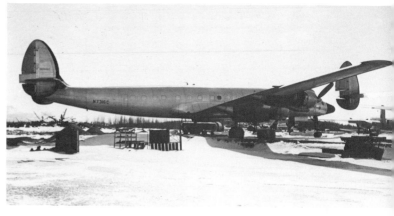

Right:
With the introduction of jet airliners, the Starliner did not last long in TWA's service. This one, (c/n 1018) N7316C, was originally with TWA but was sold off and flew with Flying 'W' Airways, Alaska Airlines Inc, and the Prudhoe Bay Oil Distributing Co, which operated out of Anchorage, Alaska. *MAP*

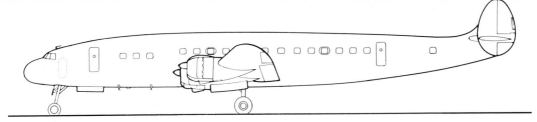

Appendices

1 Technical Data

Lockheed Constellation and Super Constellation

Model C-69 Originally military transport version of 1943. *Powerplant:* Four 2,200hp Wright Cyclone R-3350-35 18-cylinder radial engines driving 3-blade Hamilton Standard Hydromatic full-feathering propellers. *Performance:* Max speed 347mph at 20,000ft; cruising speed 275mph; landing speed 77mph; climb 1,620ft/min; range (normal) 2,400 miles; service ceiling 25,300ft. *Weights:* Empty 50,000lb; loaded (max take-off) 72,000lb. *Dimensions:* Span 123ft; length 95ft 2in; height 23ft 8in; wing area 1,650sq ft.

Model L-049 Basically a conversion of USAAF C-69, with max take-off weight increased to 86,250lb; also modified Wright engines — 2,200hp 745C18BA3s instead of BA1s.

Model L-049A As L-049 but with reinforced front wing-spar and main landing gear side-struts; max take-off weight increased to 90,000lb.

Model L-049B As L-049A but max take-off weight increased to 93,000lb, fuselage external rails incorporated and new metering pins fitted in main landing gear.

Model L-049C As L-049B but MLG drag strut damper and 15:1 elevator boost ratio included.

Model L-049D As L-049C but with reinforced inner wing and increase in max take-off weight to 96,000lb.

Model L-149 As L-049D but outer wing panels modified to incorporate fuel tanks; max take-off weight increased to 100,000lb.

Model L-649 New version with Wright 749C18BD1 engines rated at 2,500hp; revised engine cowlings (range-peel type); air conditioning installed; much improved furnishings and shock-mounting cabin walls (the first true civil Constellation), max take-off weight 94,000lb.

Model L649A As L-649 but with reinforcements to fuselage and inner wing, modified brakes and increase to max take-off weight of 98,000lb.

Model L-749 Similar to L-649A but with modified outer wing panels incorporating extra fuel tanks; max take-off weight increased to 102,000lb.

Model L-749A As L-749 but incorporated fuselage, inner wing and MLG strengthening, also modified braking system; max take-off weight up to 107,000lb.

Model L-1049 New version known as Super Constellation; increase in fuselage length by 18.4ft 8,000 to 25,000ft pressurisation; new type windscreen, redesigned cabin windows of rectangular shape; optional centre-section fuel tanks; four uprated 2,700hp Wright 975C118CB1 (R-3350-CA1) Cyclone radial engines fitted; max take-off weight 120,000lb.

Model L-1049A Became new military variant which developed into R7V-1, R7V-2, WV-1 and WV-2 (US Navy), and C-121A, VC-121B, RC-121C and RC-121D (US Air Force).

Above:
C-69 Constellation prototype (c/n 1961) seen in USAAC olive drab scheme. Allotted the military serial 43-10309, the type was designated C-69A. *Lockheed*

Model L-1049B Civil freighter version based on military L-1049A with uprated 3,250hp Wright 972TC18DA1 Turbo-Compound radial engines (R-3350-DA1); strengthened airframe to allow for max take-off weight of 130,000lb. Order for four by Seaboard and Western cancelled in favour of updated Model L-1049D.

Model L-1049C First passenger-carrying version powered by the Turbo-Compound engines; fitted with Dreyfuss-styled interior; max take-off weight increased to 133,000lb.

Model L-1049D As L-1049C but with modified wing and fuselage to allow for max take-off weight of 150,000lb as pure freighter variant with heavy-duty floor and cargo doors fitted.

Model L-1049E As L-1049C but modified to have up to 150,000lb max take-off weight capability; of 26 constructed a large proportion were converted to L-1049G standard while still on production line.

Model L-1049F Company designation for the military C-121C version of which 33 were built.

Model L-1049G Most successful and prolific of the L-1049 series, which warrants a more detailed summary of Super 'G' data (typical configuration) as follows: Update of L-1049E with Wright TC-18-DA3 Turbo-Compound radials; featured wingtip tanks which increased total fuel capacity to 6,453

Imp gal. *Performance:* Max speed 362mph; cruising speed (normal at 20,000ft) 305mph; climb (gross weight/sea level) 1,140ft/min; landing speed 99.5mph; range (still air — max fuel — full reserves) 5,100 miles, or normal range (max fuel — no reserves) 4,820 miles at 10,000ft; service ceiling 27,600ft. *Weights:* Empty (equipped) 79,000lb; loaded (max take-off) 141,700lb. *Dimensions:* Span 123ft (126ft 2in over tip tanks); length 113ft 7in (116ft 2in with radar nose); height 24ft 9in; wing area 1,650sq ft.

Model L-1249 (R7V-2) Turboprop development based on L-1049D powered by four Pratt & Whitney T-34s; four built, two remaining with US Navy and two going to US Air Force as YC-121Fs. No commercial orders.

L-1249A/1249B/1449/1549 All Lockheed projects only.

Model L-1049H Dual-purpose/convertible version of L-1049G for use as passenger and/or freighter aircraft; fitted with heavy-duty flooring and freight doors as for L-1049D; uprated 3,400hp TC-18-EA-6 Turbo-Compounds could be fitted resulting in a 140,000lb plus max take-off weight; final version of Super Constellation, the last being delivered in November 1958.

L-1649A Starliner

Production version of extra long-range transport, with basically an L-1049G fuselage married to a newly designed wing incorporating laminar flow and increased span as well as containing additional fuel. *Powerplant:* Four 3,400hp Wright R-3350-988TC-18EA-2 Turbo-Compound radials driving 3-bladed Hamilton Standard Hydromatic propellers featuring reverse pitch. *Performance:* Max speed 377mph at 18,600ft; cruising speed (normal) 290mph at 22,000ft; climb (sea level) 1,080ft/min; range (max payload) 4,940 miles; service ceiling 23,700ft. *Weights:* Empty 91,645lb; loaded (max take-off) 160,000lb. *Dimensions:* Span 150ft; length (with radar nose) 116ft 2in; height 24ft 9in; wing area 1,850sq ft.

Above:
In this picture, EC-121T serialled 54-2307, is seen at Mildenhall on 26 August 1978. *Roger P. Wasley*

Far left:
An Air France L-1049C Super Constellation (c/n 4515), F-BGNF, stands at Heathrow on a misty morning in 1958 while preparations are made to disembark her passengers. *MAP*

Left:
This taxying shot is of TWA's Super 'G' Connie (c/n 4587) N7106C. *MAP*

2 Service with Principal Airline Fleets

Trans World Airways (TWA)

C-69 (Under jurisdiction of USAAF Air Transport Command) six from 1944.

L-049 (Including military conversions from 14 machines either delivered to USAAF or on production line on VJ-Day, after which military orders cancelled): 42 entered TWA service, two of which — NX54212/4 (c/ns 1971 and 1974) — were employed on pilot training only.

L-749 12 entered service.

L-749A 28 entered service of which at least five — N6010C/12C/13C, N86521/2 (c/ns 2646, 2648, 2649, 2642 and 2653 respectively) — were built in sleeper configuration for night services.

L-1049 10 of this basic model entered service.

L-1049C Only seven are believed to have entered TWA service before the Super 'G' became available. As far as is known the c/ns were 4550, 4551, 4552, 4554, 4555, 4556 and 4557.

L-1049G 29 Super 'G's delivered to TWA.

L-1049H Just nine of this convertible passenger/cargo version entered TWA service.

L-1649A Starliner Delivery totalled 29, but of these at least 12 operated in pure freighter configuration from 1960-61.

Air France

L-049 At least four acquired for service in 1947.

L-749 14 of this version entered Air France service.

L-749A Acquisition of this modified L-749 variant totalled 10.

L-1049C 10 entered service.

L-1049G 14 Super 'G's delivered for service on long-haul routes.

L-1649A 10 Starliners went into service with the French airline.

British Overseas Airways Corporation

L-049 Put eight into service.

L-749 BOAC took delivery of five.

L-749A 12 entered service between 1953-55.

Eastern Air Lines Inc

L-049 12 taken on charge.

L-649 14 delivered.

L-749 Just seven entered service on acquisition.

L-1049 14 entered service.

L-1049C 17 delivered for long-haul routes.

L-1049G A total of 10 Super 'G's went into service.

L-1049H Eastern put five of these 'convertibles' into service.

Flying Tiger Line Inc

L-1049H This all-freighter airline purchased 21 for cargo duties only.

Below:
L-749 Constellation F-BAZU of Air France is seen here at Heathrow Airport in 1959. *MAP*

KLM (Royal Dutch Airlines)

L-049   Took delivery of six.
L-749   13 entered service.
L-749A   Acquired seven.
L-1049C   13 delivered.
L-1049G   Purchased six.
L-1049H   Just three of this passenger/cargo variant entered service.

Lufthansa

L-1049G   Took delivery of eight Super 'G's.
L-1049H   Just two entered service.
L-1649A Starliner   Only four entered service of which two — D-ALUB/AN (c/ns 1034 and 1040) — operated in cargo configuration.

Pan American World Airways Panair Do Brasil

C-69   (Under jurisdiction of USAAF Air Transport Command) one in 1945, serial 310311 (c/n 1963).
L-049   Pan Am took delivery of 29 machines, but one — N88849 (c/n 2049) — went directly to Panair do Brasil.
L-749   Just five delivered and put into service.
L-749A   Only one entered service — N9907E (c/n 2602).
L-1049   Only one Super Connie also entered Pan Am service — N6213C (c/n 4013).
L-049/149   Panair do Brasil received 11 L-049s and five L-149s (the latter being the L-049 original version with extra wing tanks fitted).

QANTAS (Australia)

L-749   Took delivery of six aircraft and flew one leased machine (c/n 2555).
L-1049C   Operated four of this version.
L-1049G   Took delivery of 10 Super 'G's.
L1049H   Just two of the passenger/freighter variant supplied to QANTAS.

Trans-Canada Air Lines Inc

L-1049C   Operated five of this version.
L-1049E/G   Flew three L-1049Es and four Super 'G's.
L-1049H   Only two of the 'convertible' Super Connie entered service.

Air India International

L-749   Took delivery of three machines.
L-749A   Just four of this version entered service.
L-1049C   Only two of this variant of Super Connie entered service.
L-1049E/G   Three L-1049Es entered service followed by five Super 'G's.

Below:
QANTAS Super 'G' (c/n 4680) VH-EAP with flaps down and engines throttled back prepares to touch down. Note the auxiliary tip-tanks. *QANTAS*

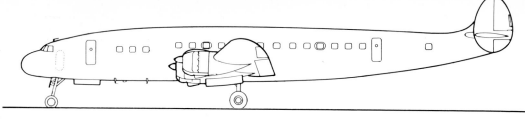

Bibliography

W. Sweetman; *A History of Passenger Aircraft*; Hamlyn, 1979

Holmes G. Anderson; *The Lockheed Constellation*; Profile No 120, Profile Publications, 1966

Peter J. Marson; *The Lockheed Constellation Series*; Air Britain

Enzo Angelucci and John Stroud; *World Encyclopedia of Civil Aircraft*; Collins/Willow, 1984

Lockheed Field Service Digest, 1957; *The Model 1649A Starliner*

Lockheed Aircraft Corp Newsbureau, publication for writers' information, mid-1950s; *The Constellation and Super Constellation*

Aeronautical Engineering Review, July 1945; Clarence L. 'Kelly' Johnson; *The Development of the Lockheed Constellation*; paper to Los Angeles Section IAS, 30.11.44

The Illustrated Encyclopedia of Aircraft Nos 113, 118, 123; Orbis Publishing, 1983-84

R. E. G. Davies; *Airlines of Latin America Since 1919*; Putnam, 1984

A. J. Jackson; *British Civil Aircraft Since 1919* Vol 3; Putnam, 1974

R. A. Saville-Sneath; *Aircraft of the United States* Vol 1; Penguin, 1945

H. J. Cooper, O. G. Thetford, D. A. Russell; *Aircraft of the Fighting Powers* Vol 4; Harborough, 1944

D. Baldry and B. Gunston; *Piston Airliners Since 1940*; Phoebus, 1980

W. Green and G. Swanborough; *The Observer's World Airlines and Airliners Directory*; Frederick Warne, 1975

J. M. Andrade; *US Military Aircraft Designations and Serials Since 1909*; Midland Counties Publications

Air Enthusiast No 14, Dec 1980-Mar 1981; Fine Scroll/Ducimus Books

Peter A. Danby; *United States Navy Serials 1941 to 1976* (3rd Ed); Merseyside Aviation Society, 1976

Right:
Another view of the first production L-1049, which began Eastern Air Lines' scheduled New York to Miami service on 17 December 1951. The de-icer boots, built integrally into the leading edges of the wings, fins and tailplane, can be clearly discerned in this picture. Propellers were of the Hamilton Standard type on EAL Super Connies, and featured fluid anti-icing as well as hydromatic and hydraulic feathering and reverse pitch.
Lockheed